WHY
PRIESTS?

ANSWERS GUIDED BY THE
TEACHING OF BENEDICT XVI

PAUL JOSEF CARDINAL CORDES

*English translation by Peter Spring
and Monsignor Anthony J. Figueiredo, STD*

 Scepter

To Pope Benedict XVI
Successor of Peter and
Convincing Herald of the Word of God
with Deep Respect

CONTENTS

Only if he is in love with Christ will the priest be able to teach his union, this intimate friendship with the divine Teacher, to all, and be able to move people's hearts and open them to the Lord's merciful love. Only in this way, consequently, will he be able to instill enthusiasm and spiritual vitality in the communities the Lord entrusts to him. Let us pray that through the intercession of Saint Jean Marie Vianney, God will give holy priests to his Church and will increase in the faithful the desire to sustain and help them in their ministry.

—*Pope Benedict's General Audience, August 5*

INTRODUCTION

୬୬

For sure we were exhausted—the group of seminarians from the "Séminaire universitaire" in Lyon. On an April evening in 1958 we had set out on the over 30 km-long hike to Ars. Leaving the city behind us, we had walked through the night, taking side roads and bypaths along the banks of the Saône. Then, the huge fields full of golden yellow blossoms had suddenly appeared to us out of the glimmering dawn light. They have remained as a vivid and unforgettable image in my mind. Soon the little town of Ars rose up before us. The town had so often been mentioned during our previous year of study in seminary—on the Place Abbé Larue on the "holy hill" of Saint Just and in the Faculty of the "Catho" in the city below. Saint Jean Marie Vianney was on the tongues of us all. Preparations for his approaching centenary (in 1959) were especially fervent in the diocese of Lyon, heralded by announcements of all kinds. We prospective priests were eager to follow in the traces of the famous Curé of Ars, of whom we had heard so much, in the little town where he had lived and worked as parish priest. So familiar were we with his name that it was almost as if he had become our contemporary.

THE HOLY CURÉ OF ARS

At first, in the early morning, we celebrated, rather sleepily, the Sunday liturgy in a large square, which had already been prepared for the approaching jubilee. Then we hastened into the center of the little town to visit the authentic relics of the past: the places consecrated by the Saint's presence. There—it was said—the time of the Saint had, as it were, stood still. Everything associated with him had been preserved. Yet the little town, devoid of any remarkable sights, soon disabused us of any sublime thoughts: the old buildings with unplastered rough stone walls; the parish house with its smoke-blackened walls and the blind window of the scarcely inhabitable kitchen with its beaten earth floor—everything was not only frugal but wretched and miserable. Not even a minimum of seemliness or luster. The whole house, on the contrary, was bare, shabby, off-putting. Equally unprepossessing was the nondescript church with its life-size plastercast figures, its sugary paintings, its open confessional, lacking even a minimum of discretion or confidentiality.

Forgiving Sins

It was especially in the confessional that Father Vianney had concentrated his service as parish priest during his time in Ars, where he spent most of his life. As his contemporaries reported, he came into the church no later than two in the morning, or in the winter around three, and heard confessions until the beginning of Mass at six. Then he was busy in the sacristy for a time. Between eight and eleven he administered the sacrament mainly to men either in the sacristy itself or in the ambulatory of the choir. He ate a few morsels for lunch. Then, in the afternoon, from two o'clock to the evening, he returned to the confessional. On average he spent some fifteen hours in the confessional each day. Abbé Dubouis, parish priest of the neighboring parish of Farein, asked him one day how he could hold out for so long in the confessional even in the freezing cold of winter, without even being able to warm his feet. "There's a good reason for that," the Curé d'Ars replied. "From All Saints to Easter my feet are so numb I don't even feel them." Though he was constantly totally exhausted by his fasting, his penitential exercises, his illnesses, and sleep deprivation, he was able to keep up this grueling schedule and these long sessions in the confessional right to the end of his life.

Jean Marie Vianney was the saint of the confessional. He rejoiced when great sinners came to him. He alternated severity with gentleness and compassion. Yet his words nearly always went to people's hearts. "Yes, if God were not so good. For He is so infinitely good," he said. He also said: "So what has the Lord done to you that you should treat Him in this way?" No wonder that he also learned to recognize the whole burden of sin. He often wept in the confessional; once, when someone asked him why, he replied: "My friend, I weep because you don't weep." "Truly, God will be so bitterly insulted," he complained on another occasion, "that one is tempted to ask him for the end of the world." Then there was his lament: "If you want to experience what sin is, you've got to come to Ars. One is at a loss to know what to do to counter it; one can only weep and pray." And lastly: "When I was young, I didn't know what evil was; it's from the mouths of sinners in the confessional that I've got to know what it is."

Suffering from Persecutions

When after visiting the church we entered the small priest's house and ascended the stairs to the curé's bedroom, we began to hear of the diabolic nocturnal attacks to which he was subject. Later, during the cause for his canonization, these were put on the record. They long filled him with dread—violent hammer blows against the outer door and the inside doors, which even the night-watchman in service at the time, André Verchère, had confirmed; the sound of galloping horses coming out of the attic; the drumbeat of military marches from the water barrel; a whole pack of rats that raced through the house and that could not be expelled even with the blows of a cudgel. On the upper floor, placed in the only inhabitable room, we also saw the bed with the traces of burning, which Jean Marie himself attributed to an attempted arson attack that the devil made on him in 1856. Due to these continuous "apparitions," persecutions evidently became less frightening to him; he had become inured to ghosts; for, after this attempted arson attack, he commented, almost bemused, to his congregation: "Since Grappin"—as he called Satan—"didn't catch the bird, he burnt its cage instead."

The fate of the Saint of Ars makes it look as if the zealous priest is the prime target of the adversary of God. The Evil One especially seems to have it in for the champion of the Gospel. Isn't that something that is found not just in the life of the Holy Curé of Ars but more widely?

The great French writer Georges Bernanos enables us to experience, and makes tangible in literary form, this inveterate hatred of priests expressed by Satan—undoubtedly not without having had in mind also the life of our Saint. For instance, in the novel *Sous le soleil de Satan* (*Under Satan's Sun*)[1] Bernanos tells the story of the rural priest Donissan struggling against Satan (a horse trader) for his own soul and that of a precocious village girl. "Clear out!" he tells the devil and manages to drive him out. Then "the horrible creature makes a leap, twirls several times in fantastic agility around himself, then as if by an irresistible impulse he takes two steps forward, stretching out both arms, like a man who tries in vain to regain his balance." Now Donissan knows that God has given him the power to vanquish evil. But the devil, who would have liked to tempt him to the abuse of this power, achieves nothing, for it is the power of the sacrament.

So, Saint Jean Marie not only had to cope with his often recounted uphill struggle through seminary to final reception of the Sacrament of Holy Orders; he needed over eight years to learn Latin, and even then he understood precious little of it after he had entered (in 1813) the Séminaire in Lyon in which the theological lectures were given in Latin. Yet it was only after he had taken orders that his trials and tribulations really started. His service as parish priest was a constant battle, a constant running of the gauntlet—not only as a result of his persecution

---

[1] For an English translation: Georges Bernanos, *Under Satan's Sun*. Translated by J.C. Whitehouse, University of Nebraska Press.

by the devil, but hardly less so by the faithful of his parish and even by his fellow-priests. He himself said the following about these first years as a priest: "I was very often slandered and combated. Oh, I had so many crosses to bear. Almost more than I could take upon myself." He skates over the fact that he made three attempts to flee and vanish from Ars—in 1840, 1847, and 1853—because he wanted to seek true holiness in seclusion. But again and again he returned to the service to which he had been called. Later he confessed that he had had to fight against the temptation to despair. Slowly he learned to forget himself and his own problems in the pursuit of total self-abnegation. As he remarked one day to Azun de Bernétas during one of his frequent visits to Ars: "A wise and good Christian is after all one who is able to support the hardship of his service with serenity and composure."

Fisher of Men

It was in this rather shocking way that the authentic contours of a saint were revealed to us seminarians—so totally shorn of the usual halo and the glittering golden frame. The ideal life of the priest—an oppressive conspiracy between troublesome parishioners and the powers of evil? So far we had seen nothing of the rest of the little town with its nondescript buildings clearly of more recent date. There, too, something quite unexpected awaited us. In a shop window were hung chronological charts of the number of pilgrims to the little town. They came to visit it even during the lifetime of the parish priest. They were listed according to annual numbers. Jean Marie received the Sacrament of Holy Orders at the age of 29 in 1815. He began his service as parish priest in this insignificant and shabby little town in the middle of nowhere in 1818. After only ten years his reputation evidently began to spread through the surrounding area. He drew people to him. They sought him out as a father confessor. Initially only some 15–20 non-locals per year were remarked. Then their number began to swell. In 1834—fifteen years after he had taken over the parish—some 30,000 pilgrims are reported to have visited the town. Nor did they come just from the local area: they came from as far afield as Belgium, England, even from America. In the last years before his death—he died on August 4, 1859—between 80,000 and 100,000 pilgrims are said to have visited the town. What on earth prompted them to travel here? They wanted only to receive the Sacrament of Penance and receive spiritual guidance from the priest; they were very far from wanting to turn the meeting with the priest into a psychoanalytical session.

To meet the needs of the growing number of pilgrims, facilities for lodgings in the town and for reaching it by public transport were created: the little town began to grow as guesthouses and hostels for pilgrims were built. A daily rail link between Lyon and Ars was introduced. Indeed, a special counter was opened just for return tickets to Father Vianney's town at the railroad station in Lyon. The tickets were good for eight days—something unheard of at the time—because, such was the pressure of pilgrims, visitors needed several days to be able to meet the parish priest.

There is ample confirmation of these details. Even at the time I found them astonishing, sensational even.

Such an influx of people eager to receive the Sacrament of Penance and be converted may be found even more irritating in our time than the parish priest's battles against the devil. For does not God's Gospel of salvation and forgiveness seem to us today something powerless, in any case incapable of arousing an echo? Something spoken into the wind and in no way attractive? Are we not already highly satisfied when we are able to hold the parish together and maintain spiritual health, or when just one or two grains of seed fall on good soil and bear fruit "a hundredfold" (Mt 13:8)?

Father Vianney as pastor can arouse hope in the skeptics of spiritual welfare, despite all the resistance from which he suffered. He embodies in a remarkable way the luminous spiritual power of the true evangelist. He was able to appeal to those seeking spiritual conversion. Or rather: he was able to reveal to contemporaries their inner unrest, to help them discover that their hearts were not resting in God and then to reach it. "Lord, even the demons are subject to us in your name," say the seventy-two appointed by the Lord, returning full of joy after their mission to Israel (Lk 10:17). Mission in Jesus' name is not powerless even in the most adverse circumstances, even when "Satan falls like lightning from heaven." If only the servant gives scope to his master, so that his presence be felt! As the Holy Curé of Ars said one day to his first biographer Alfred Monnin: "Wherever a meeting with the saints takes place, God lets himself be met through them . . ." That is a rule that holds good even when only a lower level of holiness is present and not the strikingly heroic stature of the holiness of the Curé of Ars.

THE "YEAR FOR PRIESTS"

The year 2009 marks the 150th anniversary of the death of the Holy Curé. Pope Benedict XVI proclaimed a jubilee year to mark the occasion. On March 16, 2009, addressing the members of the Congregation for the Clergy in the Vatican's Consistory Hall, he announced that he had decided to establish a special "Year for Priests" that would begin on June 19, 2009 and last until June 19, of the following year. The motivation that inspired the Holy Father to make this announcement was the living example of this Saint and his service of Christ's flock; the conviction that this man could inspire in the heart of every priest "the aspiration to moral perfection that must dwell in every authentically priestly heart." Its aim is to encourage priests "in this striving for spiritual perfection on which, above all, the effectiveness of their ministry depends." The Pope's instruction was gratefully received by many in the Church, ordained and baptized alike. The hope is that the Year for Priests may make "the importance of the priest's role and mission in the Church and in contemporary society ever more clearly perceived." For if their service, indeed their rank, may once become clear to their parishes and to the Church as a whole, thanks to a specific act of remembrance before God, all priests may be encouraged anew in their "striving for spiritual perfection."

Wind of Resistance

The "crisis of faith" is not something that has spread in the world by pessimists: the crisis exists. And because there is a "crisis of faith," there is also a "crisis of priests." This is undoubtedly due to the lack of spiritual vocations. But it's also because the media are so fond of publicizing the misdemeanors and weaknesses of priests. They relish scandals more than anything; for, in the eyes of the media, the virtuous, the good, the altruistic never make interesting headlines! Consequently, when the question of priests arises, people tend to express their apprehensions, or they turn their gaze elsewhere. Such reactions may make us all feel uncertain.

The wind of resistance, we recall, also blew into the face of Saint Jean Marie, albeit in a different way: during his studies in seminary, in the torments of his spiritual service, in his struggle against the "authorities and powers" (1 Pet 3:22). It was just on this latter battleground that Satan's hatred of the priest was shown. Though the Holy Curé was extremely skeptical of mystical phenomena, the adversary of God can almost be felt as a tangible force, as a real and frightening presence, in his life.

Yet the devil does not always show himself so openly in this way. To us "average pastors" he prefers to use more concealed, more subtle weapons. The priest is a source of irritation to the world around him if he refuses to conform to it, to adjust himself to its ways. His very existence then becomes offensive; it appears presumptuous, even arrogant, to others. Why does he segregate himself from others by his frugal lifestyle, his devotional practices, his celibacy? Instead of all that—so go the more recent accusations leveled against him—he ought to conform, incorporate himself in the "working team of full-time pastors," and no longer hold onto his own "professional profile," artificially separated from the laity by his clerical rank.

Georges Bernanos vividly describes in his novel *Journal d'un curé de campagne* (Diary of a Country Priest) the sufferings of the priest who does not wish to conform. He observes under wholly different social circumstances the same social pressure that today weighs down the young priest under a sense of alienation. To the local aristocrat and landowner, M. le Comte Dumouchel, after the death of his wife, the presence of this new pastor in the parish is especially antipathetic. During a bruising encounter with the curé he can no longer control his dislike and contempt for the priest: "'Your kind'—he paused a moment—'your kind, as well as your habits, seem to me to pose a real danger to this parish,' says the lord of the parish, taking his leave and finally turning his back on the priest."[2]

Had not the "country priest" sought to be useful to the people and earn their goodwill? It's not as if he had been faultless and had given his parish no cause to feel hostility towards him. Just as the Church has been characterized by weaknesses and sins ever since its first apostle Peter, so its ordained servants have throughout history caused offense and discredited their holy office. But their rejection, sometimes so well-founded, is not the issue here. We speak now of those who out of pride or an overestimate of themselves deny their need for redemption. This happens when someone refuses to perceive his own ungodliness; when his arrogance covers over his sins—according to the axiom of Nietzsche. "'I've done that,' says my memory. 'I cannot have done that,' says my pride. Finally the memory gives in." M. le Comte Dumouchel admits no need for redemption or forgiveness.

Hostility towards the priest clearly grows when the need for redemption is ignored or disputed. The service of the priest will then come to resemble the way of redemption of Christ himself. The French author has described how the process takes shape in an almost demonic way: "Hatred of priests is one of man's

---

[2] For an English translation: Georges Bernanos, *The Diary of a Country Priest*. Introduction by Rémy Rougeau. Translated by Pamela Morris, New York: Carroll & Graf Publishers, 2002, here p. 195.

deepest feelings, also one of the least well known. That it is as old as the species itself cannot be doubted, but it is only in our time that it has increased to an almost astonishing degree of refinement and subtlety. For the decline and eradication of other forms of authority have turned the priest—however closely bound up he apparently is with the life of the community—into a being as unique and as unclassifiable as any of the magic and venerable sages that the ancient world kept locked in the innermost cells of temples, like holy beasts that associate only with the gods." So writes Bernanos in another novel about the life of a priest *Monsieur Ouine* on which he worked for almost ten years and which was not published till 1940.

Indifference

Antipathy to the priest may today be less perceptible and less painful than the creeping indifference with which his service is regarded by contemporaries—in our secularized society and in a Church in which faith is weak. The feudal lord M. le Comte Dumouchel wishes to expel the "country curé" from his sphere of authority, because he is found to be disturbing and annoying; he doesn't want him to meddle in his private affairs. It's more modern now to pose the question, "Why bother to have priests at all?"; and to detach the service of the priest, whether objectively or theoretically, from the sacrament of his ordination. Or, instead of that, there are those who suggest that individual activities in the Church should be assigned to specialized professionals (or charisms), thus rendering the Sacrament of Holy Orders and the ordained ministry redundant.

Alternatively, the priest is incorporated in a pastoral team, responsibility for whose direction is assigned to a pastoral area ("community of parishes"). This team consists of priests, pastoral assistants, and other laity. The result is administration according to a sociological model. The delegation of pastoral care to "experts" reduces the chance of arousing or promoting faith among the community through personal contacts, personal witness, and greater trust. The priest admittedly is still required for some specific "functions." But the Church no longer grows from the Sacrament of Ordination that was specifically founded for the "building up of the community." And so the identity of the ordained is gradually eroded.

The participation of all the baptized in the mission of the Church, which Vatican II had rightly called for, thanks to the rediscovery of the common priesthood of all the faithful (1 Pet 2:5ff.), is unfortunately misunderstood in some new pastoral models. The effect is damaging: secularization takes hold. The biblically founded anchoring of the dignity of the Christian in God is democratically usurped; equality is no longer the equality of everyone before God, each with his or her different responsibility in the mission of the Church, but is forced into a uniform model of conformism which lumps together and homogenizes all the Church's pastoral services. In some places, especially in Europe, the pastoral councils prescribed or at least encouraged by the Second Vatican Council have emancipated themselves, turned themselves into mini-parliaments, and assumed the function of decision-making bodies. The grace of ordination with which the ordained ministry is armed is eliminated. What essentially differentiates the ministerial or hierarchical priesthood from the common priesthood of all the faithful (cf. Constitution of the Church *Lumen Gentium*, no. 10) dwindles or vanishes in the consciousness of the faithful.

For such dubious developments a few Swiss dioceses have acted as pacesetters in the German-speaking world. A few years ago they dispensed with the independent responsibility of a priest for providing the pastoral care of a parish, reformed the territorial parish organization, turning parishes into "pastoral units" and placing them under the control of a "pastoral team" to which a priest also belongs. In the "pastoral unit" it is no longer the ordained minister who assumes the leadership, but the male or female person appointed by the bishop (Statutes for the Bishopric of Saint Gallen of 2002). In Germany, too, various dioceses are moving in the same direction—for instance, the bishopric of Aachen. There the program is called "pastoral care in groups of parishes" (since 2005). "The parish council participates in the administration of the parish." A priest admittedly belongs to this administration, but it exercises "joint responsibility." It's no longer a question of a "ministerial priest" who differs essentially and in degree in his mission by virtue of the Sacrament of Holy Orders he has received: instead of that, the talk is of "ordained services" and "non-ordained services."

Can anyone be surprised, therefore, if the very foundations of the clergy's specific identity begin to wobble under the feet of this or that priest; or if the number of vocations to the priesthood has dramatically fallen in various parts of the world?

A "Sentences Commentary"

It is through theology that structural and existential pastoral problems and pitfalls are discovered in the most convincing way. The following analyses are offered in this light. They treat the various fundamental questions of Church doctrine on the priest's mission. Their aim is to indicate, and raise awareness of, the doctrinal roots of his service, so that the priest's identity may be reinforced in the ordained minister himself; so that the faithful may lose whatever reservations they may have about the priest's ministry, or its need; and, especially, so that young men who feel they have a vocation will no longer doubt its objective indispensability.

Each field of investigation will be introduced by "*sententiae*" from the rich storehouse of the teachings of our present Pope. Over the years Cardinal Ratzinger, later to become Pope Benedict XVI, expressed his opinions on many current theological issues. He has, not least, a loving eye for the opportunities and needs of priests. In the "commentary" that follows I will then try to analyze the formulations found in these short excerpts from his teachings. The theological genre of the "sentences commentary" was familiar in medieval scholasticism and has long retained its value in the history of philosophy and theology. The interpretations offered as commentary on the texts from Benedict XVI's teachings cited at the head of the chapters in large part present my own reflections, which have been developed over the last few years as a commentary on Vatican II's Decree on the Ministry and Life of Priests (*Presbyterorum Ordinis*). Fresh references to the Sacrament of Holy Orders are suggested not least by the Pope's intention to institute a "Year for Priests" to mark the jubilee of the Holy Curé of Ars.

Pope Benedict XVI has again and again urged that the Second Vatican Council be the measure and criterion for the Church's thought and action. Immediately after his election as Pope, addressing the College of Cardinals in the Sistine Chapel on 20 April 2005, Benedict expressed his determination "to continue to put the Second Vatican Council into practice, following in the footsteps of my Predecessors and in faithful continuity with the 2,000-year tradition of the Church." As theologian he cultivates a "hermeneutic of reform" that deepens the venerable and unaltered doctrine of the Church and yet formulates it in such a way that it corresponds to the requirements of our time.

The publication being presented here has the title "Why Priests?" Old and new elements from the pen of the Holy Father and my own reflections added to them[3] are intended to provide an answer to this question. They are aimed at identifying elements that may raise awareness of the status of priests and give them a new consciousness of their mission, based on God's call. For priests are irreplaceable. Pope John Paul II described this in his first Letter to Priests on the Occasion of Holy Thursday 1979 using moving words based on rich personal experience:

---

[3] In various ways I have devoted my attention to aspects of the theology and spirituality of the ministerial priesthood. My first contribution in this field was a publication devoted to an historical and exegetical study of Vatican II's Decree on the Ministry and Life of Priests (*Presbyterorum Ordinis*): *Sendung zum Dienst. Exegetisch-Historische und systematische Studien zum Konzilsdekret 'Von Dienst und Leben der Priester,'* Frankfurt, 1972; Cardinal Karl Lehman referred to the continuing validity of this book in his introduction to P. Hünerman (ed.), *Das Zweite Vatikanische Konzil und die Zeichen der Zeit heute*, Freiburg, 2006, 11–28, here note 12.

Dear Brothers: you who have borne 'the burden of the day and the heat' (Mt 20:12), who have put your hand to the plough and do not turn back (cf. Lk 9:62), and perhaps even more those of you who are doubtful of the meaning of your vocation or of the value of your service: think of the places where people anxiously await a priest, and where for many years, feeling the lack of such a priest, they do not cease to hope for his presence. And sometimes it happens that they meet in an abandoned shrine, and place on the altar a stole which they still keep, and recite all the prayers of the Eucharistic liturgy; and then, at the moment that corresponds to the transubstantiation a deep silence comes down upon them, a silence sometimes broken by a sob ... so ardently do they desire to hear the words that only the lips of a Priest can efficaciously utter! How they desire Eucharistic Communion, in which they can share only through the ministry of a priest, just as they also so eagerly wait to hear the divine words of pardon: *Ego te absolvo a peccatis tuis!* [I absolve you from your sins]. How deeply do they feel the absence of a priest among them! (no. 10).

I

ORIGINS

BIBLICAL ROOTS

What is special to theology is that it addresses itself to what we have not discovered ourselves and what can be for us, precisely as a result of such study, the foundation of life, because it precedes us and supports us, in other words is greater than our own capacity for thought. The way of theology is effectively described by the axiom *"credo ut intelligam"*: I believe, I accept the presupposition, the preordained truth of a sign, so that through it and in it I may gain access to the just life, to the right understanding of myself. But that means that theology, by its very nature, presupposes *auctoritas*. That theology exists at all is only by virtue of the fact that its truths are able to break into the closed circle of our own thought, and that a hand is so to say stretched out to our thought: a hand that draws it upwards and elevates it beyond its own inherent strengths. Without this presupposition, which is always more than what the self itself is able to think of and which is never reduced to a merely personal attainment, theology would not exist.

But now another question is posed: What does this presupposition look like—this sign that conducts human thought onto the right path and shows it the way? In the first place we can say that this authority is a word. This is wholly logical, if we consider the matter: for the word comes from understanding and wishes to lead to understanding. The sign given to the human mind in the search for meaning coincides, reasonably, with the word. In the process of science thought precedes the word; it is translated into words. But here, where our own thought fails, the Word is thrown towards us like a lifeline from the eternal wisdom, the Word in which a splinter of its splendor is concealed—as much as we can support, as much as we need, as much as human words can comprehend. To recognize the significance of this Word, to understand this Word— that is the root cause of theology, which can never be completely lacking even in the life of faith of the simplest believer.

—*Cardinal Joseph Ratzinger, Words of Thanks for the degree Doctor honoris causa at the Theological Faculty of the University of Navarre in Pamplona, January 31, 1998*

THE NEW ECCLESIOLOGY OF VATICAN II

The Second Vatican Council (1962–1965) was undoubtedly the major event in the life of the Church in the last century. Although over fifty years have elapsed since its conclusion, its teachings have so far not been completely absorbed into the life of the Church. In its reception into the consciousness and action of the Church, various observers think they can continue its theological theses as it were in a vacuum, without taking into consideration the process that led to their formulation. They propose to reinterpret the Council by isolating and using certain statements of the conciliar documents to promote or support their own ideas. They start out from the assumption that the conciliar Fathers in reality meant something rather different from what was formulated at the time. They thus use the conciliar resolutions to demand a radical theological upheaval, a fresh start. The Holy Father Pope Benedict has on various occasions urged the teachings of Vatican II be placed in the context of the Church's tradition and warned against reading into the Council a breach with the apostolic transmission of the doctrine of the Church.[1]

---

[1] For instance in his first Christmas address to the College of Cardinals and staff of the Roman Curia (December 22, 2005).

The theological and pastoral statements of the bishops at Vatican II, and the intentions that lie behind them, can best be interpreted if one looks at the process of their formulation. We have learned to appreciate the positive gains to be drawn from the history of the redaction of a text from the exegesis of the Old and New Testaments. Many verses of Holy Scripture can be better understood if we know and attend to the various stages of their writing; for instance, in the New Testament by distinguishing what Jesus himself said (*"ipsissima vox"*) from the testimonies of the young Church and those of the Evangelists. This method of exegesis should also be helpful in illuminating the conciliar texts. Assuming we really desire to trace the spirit of the Council, this method should be adopted. For example, in the process of drafting the Dogmatic Constitution on the Church *Lumen Gentium* (*LG*), the method is revealing both in clarifying the ecclesiology expressed and the theological movements that predominated at the time. In the context of this study, it goes without saying that special attention will be paid to the Church's ordained ministry.

De-Christianized West

An aspect of particular importance for the conciliar understanding of the ordained ministry is the heightened sensitivity in the field of pastoral theology that developed in France in the first half of the last century. In the years between 1932 and 1937 the Dominican Father Yves Congar examined the concept of "mission" and contributed to its understanding in the Church's thought. He wanted especially to offer theological insights and clarifications to Catholic Action in France. He sought a dynamic theology that would give new impulses. The publication of a small book, *La France, pays de mission* (France, mission country),[2] gave an additional impulse. The community of all the baptized was called to open itself to the task of mission, and to the preaching

---

[2] The two chaplains of the Young Christian Workers (CAJ) Henri Godin and Y. Daniels delivered a severe blow to the myth of Catholic France with their book published in 1943.

of the Gospel to the whole world. The laity thereby received further theological affirmation for their role in the firm structure of the ministerial Church that was their due because of baptism.

The French Catholic theologian and Dominican priest Marie-Dominique Chenu supplemented Yves Congar's perspective. He underlined the reciprocity between mission and world: there is not only a mission-conscious Church that brings her message to the world, but also a world that through changing situations leads to the introduction of new emphases in the Church's message. In July 1947, during an annual assembly of the *Mission de France*, the phrase was coined of the Church "*en état de mission*": the Church in a permanent missionary state. The task of mission thus underlined primarily involves the missionary who goes to foreign lands to proclaim the Gospel of Christ; but the de-Christianized society of the "Christian West" also needs witnesses of the Gospel, and to fulfill this task, the ordained ministers of the Church are neither exclusively equipped nor able—either then nor now—to accomplish it alone.

In this way the dimension of salvation history was restored to the concept of *missio*: the baptized and confirmed were involved in the transmission of God's Word. They all have a part to play in the Lord's mission. At the same time, the dependence of each Christian life on the Gospel does not mean that the concrete form of participation in mission is unalterable, that it necessarily remains the same forever, or that it has been historically 'petrified' once and for all. On the contrary, the call that arises in the here and now constantly modifies and renews the one and only mission that springs from the Gospel.

The Authority of Holy Scripture

All these contents are implicit in the concept of *missio* as Vatican II uses it, with the result that it gains a high value in the Dogmatic Constitution on the Church *Lumen Gentium* and the Decree on the Ministry and Life of Priests (*Presbyterorum Ordinis*). Yves Congar described how this concept was received in the conciliar documents as follows: "In general Vatican II has shown that the Church springs from the tasks assigned to her by God, they in turn founded in the action of the Trinity. From this divine source the Church gains an essentially missionary existence; the aim for which she was instituted is the dissemination of herself by the communication of the Gospel to the ends of the earth."[3]

This process might be summed up as follows: The sending of the Son in the economy of salvation derives its origin from his immanent relationship within the Trinity and is continued in the life of the Church. The Church, however, sent out into the world in this way, has the task of bringing the Gospel to every society and culture with the participation of *all* her members, constantly illuminated anew by the circumstances and situations of time and place.

The conciliar Decree on the Ministry and Life of Priests (*Presbyterorum Ordinis: PO*) remains the unsurpassable foundation for our time for the exposition of the priest's mission. It is a very powerful, indeed fundamental, text, in which the bishops from all over the world, who assembled for the Council in Rome, gave us reliable criteria for our service as priests. Its theological background is clearer to someone who has first examined the process of the drafting of the Dogmatic Constitution on the Church *Lumen Gentium* (*LG*), on which *PO* was later in part based and on whose theology it draws.

Having initially planned to treat the "Hierarchy" in chapter two of this Constitution and to defer the "People of God" to the following chapter, the Council Fathers then decided, after intensive discussions, to reverse this order. The description of the People of God was thus given priority in the Constitution; for it was rightly pointed out that the Council's theological deliberations regarding the members of the Church equally concerned all the laity as well as the ordained ministers. So in *LG* the chapter

---

[3] 'Le Sacerdoce du Nouveau Testament,' in J. Frisque/Y. Congar (eds.) *Le Decret* "Presbyterorum Ordinis" *et* "Optatam Totius." Paris, 1968, 243.

on the "People of God" (Chapter II) comes before the chapter on "The Church is Hierarchical" (Chapter III).

This same logic of the Constitution on the Church is also retained in the Decree on Priests. Before it speaks more specifically of the Ministry of Priests, it refers to the common mission of the whole Church (in Chapter I: "The Priesthood in the Church's Mission"). It begins its theological exposition of the priest's identity with the following words:

> The Lord Jesus 'whom the Father consecrated and sent into the world' (Jn 10:36), makes his whole Mystical Body sharer in the anointing of the Spirit wherewith he has been anointed: for in that Body all the faithful are made a holy and kingly priesthood, they offer spiritual sacrifices to God through Jesus Christ, and they proclaim the virtues of him who has called them out of the darkness into his admirable light. Therefore there is no such thing as a member that has not a share in the mission of the whole Body. Rather, every single member ought to reverence Jesus in his heart and by the spirit of prophecy give testimony of Jesus (no. 2).

☙ Mission of All the Baptized

The Gospel of Saint John cited here repeats on several occasions that the mission of the disciples emanates from the Lord himself (e.g., Jn 20:21). And in this mission we should never forget that Jesus speaks in his capacity as the one chosen by the Father above all others. For this reason the mission cannot be understood as being limited or addressed just to the "twelve apostles"; on the contrary, it should be understood as being extended to the first Christian community as a whole:

> I sent you to reap that for which you did not labor; others have labored, and you have entered into their labor (Jn 4:38).

> As thou didst send me into the world, so I have sent them into the world (Jn 17:18).

Jesus said to them again: 'Peace be with you. As the Father has sent me, even so I send you' (Jn 20:21).

The narrower interpretation of John 20:21, and hence the limitation of the task of mission to the Church's ordained ministers, also seems inappropriate if one compares the Johannine conception of the salvific event with that of Luke. For John there is a direct link between Cross, Resurrection, and the descent of the Spirit; the disciples' meeting with the Risen Lord instantly transmits also his Spirit. According to Luke's Acts of the Apostles, on the other hand, the Spirit does not descend on the disciples till fifty days after Easter and assigns them the task of pursuing Christ's mission as the Church. "It is truly with the descent of the Spirit that the Church comes into the world. [. . .] And at the same time the Church is sent into the world. The power of Pentecost, that raises her up, is not to her own glory, but distinguishes the start of a mission that extends through the length and breadth of the world and of history: to the ends of the earth, to the end of time, to the return of the Son of Man."[4] Luke is far from supposing this mission to be reserved for 'ministers,' and this—John often comes close to the tradition of Luke—can be an interpretational help to us in our reflection on the passage cited above. For it is not only the Eleven, but, according to Acts 1:15, 120 persons who belong to the community blessed by the gift of the Holy Spirit. And Luke reports yet further episodes in which the Spirit descends among gatherings of disciples: the gathering of brothers after the release of Peter and John (Acts 4:31), the house of Cornelius (10: 44–46), the group of disciples gathered by Paul in Ephesus (19:6): to all of these the Spirit is granted and by being filled with the Spirit they gain in strength to assume the task of mission and witness.

So from the one same Spirit spring many different gifts. Through the Spirit by which God founds the Church's mission, He also inspires his followers to undertake a variety of tasks.

---

[4] Yves Congar, *La Pentecôte*. Paris, 1956, 117.

Being sent on mission cannot therefore be interpreted as something confined to the apostles or as a special attribute of the apostolic ministry. Precisely from the New Testament foundation of the faith we can draw the conclusion that, in spite of all possible differences in responsibility, the community of the People of God gathered in the Church as a whole is chosen for mission and laid under an obligation to engage in mission. That is why we must never lose sight of the lasting danger of the concept of Church and of mission being totally taken over by the ministry for itself. Again and again through the centuries the error has prevailed of identifying the Church founded by Christ with the narrow circle of the Church's ministers—whether among the ministers themselves (privileges), or among their critics ("ministerial Church"). That the Church's mission belongs to *all* the baptized has been repeatedly suppressed as a result, and the misunderstanding fostered that her ordained ministers alone are sent to perform the ministry of salvation.

The concept of "mission—*missio*," on the other hand, can only be properly understood if it is enriched with the significance attributed to it in the New Testament. So long as this guides theology, then both the aforementioned states—"the common priesthood of the faithful and the ministerial or hierarchical priesthood" (cf. *LG* 10)—assume their rightful places. Any participation of the laity in the mission of the Church, indeed the mission of the Church herself, would be doomed today if it were to be equated exclusively with the task entrusted to the hierarchy. *Missio*, i.e., transmitting and giving witness to the truth of the Gospel, is—to quote Yves Conger once again—"entrusted to the whole Church: it is the calling of the people of God. [...] And *within* this mission of the whole Church the role of the hierarchy must be defined, but it is not on that basis that the mission (of the Church) must be defined." It would in fact be disastrous if the biblical rediscovery of baptism and of the missionary task incumbent on the whole Church were to be gambled away through confining of the task of mission to the ministerial priesthood:

for it was in the concept of mission that an expression was found that would define the Church's task as entrusted to *all* her members. This concept was rediscovered on account of the laity; and it is precisely the laity who would once again be excluded if this same expression were to be used to define what is specific to the hierarchical office in the Church.

Vatican II's rediscovery of the "common priesthood of all the faithful"—the classical reference to "a chosen race, a royal priesthood, a holy nation" in the First Letter of Peter (2:5–10) is one of the most quoted biblical verses in the conciliar documents—entered into the Church with powerful impulses of renewal.[5] Since then, most of these have also found their canonical place in the Church. World Youth Days, for instance, are above all the result of the commitment and dedication of the new movements and groups in the Church. And these latter show the error of those who had hoped for an increase of vocations to the priesthood not by making the case for it, but by depreciating the laity's responsibility: on the contrary, it is precisely in the new ecclesial movements, often founded by the "merely baptized," that many spiritual vocations are being born and nurtured.

MISSION AS MINISTERIAL RESPONSIBILITY IN THE CHURCH

Despite this crucial widening of the concept of "mission," it goes without saying that in examining its field of importance the special role of the ministerial priesthood should not be submerged. Postconciliar enthusiasm about "co-responsibility" and "councils" has sometimes misunderstood the lay responsibility drawn from the Bible as a new democracy in the Church. Yet all power in the Church does not come from the people, from below: for the freedom, equality, and brotherhood of the common priesthood

---

[5] See further Paul Josef Cordes, *Nicht immer das alte Lied. Neue Glaubensanstöße der Kirche.* Paderborn, 1999.

come from above; their indispensable guarantor is God himself. It is God—to quote 1 Peter 2 again—who "has called you out of darkness into his marvelous light" (v. 9). It is God who has turned the "holy priesthood" into "God's own people" and in whom "you have received mercy" (v. 10). Only those who forget God can misconceive the priest as an equal among equals (*primus inter pares*) or even as an executive organ called to implement the decisions taken by votes in the various pastoral councils set up within the Church.

For the New Covenant being sent—expressed by the Greek term *apostellein*, meaning "to send forth"—denoted those within the circle of disciples who were invested by the Risen Lord with particular responsibility for the young community. A characteristic of ministerial office within the Church is therefore the act of sending forth itself: it is this that qualifies the minister. Clearly what is meant in the mission to be a minister, and assume ministerial responsibility in the community, is something characteristic of the general mission but with greater intensity. An exegetical examination of the foundations of ministry in the Church will help us to gain further insights.

That Jesus during his public ministry gathered a group of followers (or disciples) around him is undisputed. This phenomenon of the calling to follow in his footsteps has more recently been traced back by exegetes to the indisputable "messianic" authority of Jesus. This authority of Christ would be misunderstood if it were thought to be on a par with the usual rabbinical authority at the time. For the way Jesus understood himself differs not only in degree, but also in kind, from the traditional form of the education, teaching, and life of the Jewish rabbinate. In Jesus the teacher-pupil relationship is not established on the pupil's initiative (cf. Mk 5:19); rather, it is Jesus who acts by virtue of his own authority (Mk 1:16–20). The persons called by him do not enter into the academic world of theoretical learning, of the kind experienced in the rabbinical schools (entry into which was never described by the verb "to follow"). Following Jesus' call means, instead, the *sequela Christi*: it means following in his footsteps, in both a literal and metaphorical sense, following him in his itinerant life and sharing his homeless, insecure, indeed, endangered destiny (cf. Mt 8:20, Lk 9:58).

Those who see Jesus' actions in the context of the model of apocalyptic prophecy, or in that of the violent fundamentalism of the Zealots, also diminish, or underestimate, the calling of the disciples; for, although Jesus' call no doubt contains charismatic and eschatological elements, this Messiah does not initiate any popular movement (Mk 8:11–13; Mk 16:1–4); repudiates any form of violent enthusiasm (Lk 9: 51–56); and particularly tries to win *individuals* for his following (Mt 10:37ff.; Mk 8:34). Jesus is unique both in his struggle against the powers of evil (Lk 11:20; 10:18) and in his associating with tax collectors and sinners (Mk 2:16f.). For a long time liberal exegesis tried to describe or connote Jesus' unparalleled consciousness of his own mission, which all the synoptic Gospels trace back to his absolute messianic authority (Mk 1:22–27; Mt 7:29; cf. Lk 4:32–36), by labeling him as a charismatic figure characterized by the eschatological preoccupations of his time. But, more recently, this classification, too, was thrown into doubt by the recognition that Jesus, by his very nature, remains in the last analysis incommensurable and so basically all attempts at a phenomenological or sociological classification collapse. Quite justifiably therefore the phenomenon of the ineffable authority of Jesus is central to the more recent discussion of the historical Jesus. It cannot be better described than by the word "messianic."

The Circle of the Twelve

Most exegetes express the view that Jesus, before his death, created an inner circle among his followers to which twelve disciples belonged. These twelve lived with the Lord; they listened to his words and learned from him. According to the testimony of the synoptic Gospels, Jesus finally invested them with his mission to proclaim the arrival of the "kingdom of God" (Mk 6:7–13;

Lk 10:1ff.). The Evangelist Luke confirms the special position and authority of the disciples. "He who hears you hears me, and he who rejects you rejects me, and he who rejects me rejects him who sent me" (10:16): here a systematic, and not only a selective, relationship of the disciples to Jesus is expressed.

The call of the disciples by the historical Jesus assumed a second dimension after his Passion and Resurrection: the mission that had perhaps initially been limited in time now became, for the group of the twelve, a special and lasting one. There is no doubt that at least the young post-Easter community gave a timeless eschatological horizon to the sending out of the disciples by Jesus.

To help us understand the Church's ministry it remains significant that the inner circle goes back to Jesus' initiative. Membership in the inner circle of disciples—in contrast to the rabbinate—was dependent not on the choice made by the disciples themselves, but on their personal calling by Jesus. The Evangelist Mark thus tells us that the Twelve were called by the power of Jesus into a new identity; this was also expressed by the new surnames he gave to his disciples (Mk 3:13–19).

When Jesus himself created this inner circle, he combined with it a specific purpose in the history of salvation: the number twelve would be important for the eschatological realization of his work of salvation, for with it Jesus linked the promise that God had made to the [twelve tribes of the] children of Israel and that rested in the history of Israel. The handing over of the power of judgment to the disciples shows something similar; their appointment entailed a high responsibility for the coming kingdom and invested them with a kind of ministerial character vis-à-vis those over whom they were called to sit in judgment: "You are those who have continued with me in my trials; as my father appointed a kingdom for me, so do I appoint for you that you may eat and drink at my table in my kingdom, and sit on thrones judging the twelve tribes of Israel" (Lk 22: 28–30).

While the promise of authority given by the earthly Jesus to his disciples is sometimes only indirectly implied, the words of the Risen Lord express in an unequivocal manner the promise of Christ's sovereign omnipotence and dignity. All the Evangelists remark that it is the Risen Lord who finally admits his disciples to his full authority ("All authority in heaven and earth has been given to me") (Mt 28:18; Mk 16:15–18; Lk 24:47f.; Jn 20:23). The sending forth of the witnesses—"Go, therefore, and make disciples of all nations" (Mt 28:19)—is inconceivable without the Easter event. Nonetheless, we must recognize that there is no unbridgeable gulf between the earthly Jesus and his sending forth of the disciples on the one side and the words of the Risen Lord professing "all authority in heaven and earth" on the other.

Witness and its Challenge

With their designation as witnesses a further important factor that distinguishes the fully empowered disciples is touched on. Other than the writings of John, it is especially the Evangelist Luke who draws attention to this fact. In so doing, he defines the concept of witness and suggests that the witness is not only someone who has encountered the reality of the Risen Lord and can testify to it; with even greater emphasis than Matthew, Luke establishes a very close link between the witness and the life of the earthly Jesus. In Luke's view the essential condition of eligibility to bear witness is knowledge of Jesus' earthly existence, his resurrection, and ascension to heaven (Acts 1:21). His theological sketch of the epochs in the history of salvation leads him to demand that the witness be someone who also had direct experience of the works and teachings of Jesus of Nazareth. Through this theological formulation, "being a witness" is limited to a specific circle of persons. Luke, in his theological understanding, thus reaches the conclusion that the Twelve alone can be "witnesses of the Resurrection" in the full sense, in other words, witnesses of the Christ they had seen again with their own eyes and of his identity with the historical Jesus. So Luke understands the apostles as witnesses of the Resurrection—though without that implying that the witnesses of the Resurrection necessarily all became apostles.

It is especially in Luke's two New Testament books that the character of service is emphasized as an essential qualification of the apostle. Though he expresses with particular clarity the relation between the Resurrection of Jesus and the central task of the apostle, as we pointed out above, it is in Luke's view the celebration of the Jewish Pasch that gathered together the circle of the "apostles" in a significant way (Lk 22:14) and that should from an anticipatory perspective, be regarded as "the appointment to the apostolate" (Lk 22:28–30). The Evangelist thus underlines that the task for which Jesus prepares his disciples is essentially one of service and that this receives its model in the actions of Jesus himself; the Greek term *diakonia* is the keyword for our understanding of this.

Ministerial Calling in the Room of the Last Supper

Diakonia originally meant service at table. It was precisely in this activity that Jews found the most humble form of serving. The meaning of *diakonos* thus converges with that of *doulos* = servant. The synoptic Gospels show by their choice of words that there are indeed correspondences between both words (Lk 17:7–9).

These two words are repeatedly employed by the synoptic Gospels; they are used to denote the sociological order laid down by Jesus for his disciples. Both words are adopted by the Evangelist Luke in his account of the Last Supper: "A dispute also arose among them, which of them was to be regarded as the greatest. And he said to them, 'The kings of the Gentiles exercise lordship over them, and those in authority over them are called benefactors. But not so with you; rather, let the greatest among you become as the youngest, and the leader as one who serves'" (Lk 22:24–26). So it is in this context that we need to investigate the nature of service as the qualification of the apostle in the New Testament.

That absolute authority in the New Covenant is given to those invested with it for purposes of service is of crucial importance. A distinguishing and particular aspect of it remains the "opposite side of the coin," i.e., the burden, even the humiliation, of service. Since it is participation in the special authority of Jesus, this authority causes the servant's humble abnegation in following the same path as his Lord. The expressions used by Luke ("the greatest," "the leader") suggest that what the Evangelist especially had in mind is leaders of communities. Apart from the fact that such leaders of communities really do exist and are needed, what is particularly stressed here is that these men (the greatest and leaders) recognize their preferral as carrying with it an obligation to serve: "the leader [is] one who serves" (22:26).

Luke, in his chapter on the Last Supper, also transmits Jesus' words, from which he deduces the motive and criterion for being able to perform the task of leadership, a role at once paradoxical and necessary: "I am among you as one who serves" (22:27). Jesus, by his example, embodies both aspects: that of leader and that of servant. For these words recorded by Luke hardly refer to scattered individual phenomena from Jesus' life. On the contrary, the lowly service of the foot-washing (Jn 13:1ff.) and the role of service that the Lord depicted for himself on the day of the fulfillment of the Kingdom of God (Lk 12:37) suggest that we have here a fundamental feature of Jesus' special way of teaching and exhibiting his greatness. So, according to the example of Jesus, ordained ministers not only have the obligation to serve at table *in persona Christi*, but what is expected of them is a diaconic life that should characterize *all* their actions. The Evangelist Mark enables us to gauge the whole extent of this service: with reference to the fourth "song of the servant" in the Book of Isaiah (53:10f.) Jesus determines self-oblation as the final expression of his service: "For the Son of man also came not to be served but to serve, and to give his life as a ransom for many" (Lk 10:45). Here lies the objective foundation for understanding Jesus' teaching on service in the account of the Last Supper: it is inseparably bound up with the ransom he announces, with the moment of interpretation, and with the anticipation, both real and symbolic, of his redemptive death.

Hans Urs von Balthasar underlined the depths to which this descent into service of the disciples and of the specific emissary of Christ must go: "Christ *is* Lord and yet lowers himself to the position of servant, and honor is due to him for both. [...] But the servant [the ordained minister] is *a priori* a 'bondsman' [*Knecht*], and when he places himself in the last place of those serving, he does nothing particular to be entitled to honor for his own sake. [...] So there is no dialectical way for the Christian servant [...] to deduce from the abasement of service any new claim for superiority and distinction."

In the New Covenant, service would "not really be in the sign of Christ, if the ministry performed did not participate in the structure of his single ministry, which has its essence in the fact that the whole person is expended and consumed for the ministry. [...] Is it, then, so remarkable that the Lord's whole concern in equipping his apostles for their ministry, especially that of Peter the rock [*der Felsenmann*], should begin with humility? [...] Rightly understood: the phenomenon of ministerial de-personalization in the New Testament can only be comprehended as the minister's supreme effort to give to ministry all that he has been given; and this self-oblation, which is perfect love, is only produced through grace, by following the cross, which is the path of humiliation. [...] The role of the Catholic priest as a willing tool derives from that of Christ, and leads inexorably to the Cross. Peter was to be schooled mercilessly in this."[6]

---

[6] Hans Urs von Balthasar, 'Priesterliche Existenz,' in: idem, *Sponsa Verbi*. Einsiedeln, 1961, 388–433, here 397–400.

CHARACTER OF SERVICE ACCORDING TO CHRIST'S EXAMPLE

The necessary connection between ministerial functions and the character of service, which must be deduced from Luke, is repeated in the history of the choice of the new apostle Matthias (Acts 1:15–26). Twice the task of the apostle is described with the word *diakonia* (1:17, 25). Even if the concept tends to become ossified in the formal description of office, here the term's double mention and its link with the official term for the apostolic ministry (*apostolos*, 1:25f.) shows that it was Luke's purpose to preserve the example of Jesus as prescriptive, as *norma normans* for this service.

Whoever investigates the New Testament statements on mission must necessarily see the ordained minister in the Church as someone who is not outside, or segregated from, the mission of the people of God as a whole, still less competing against it. Quite the opposite is shown by the New Testament passages in which the mission shared by the people is described as apostolic or ministerial. So the call to mission through ministry does not form part of the basic understanding of being a Christian. When an individual is invested with the role of ordained minister, his personal mission is intensified and henceforth distinguished by the new obligation and strength that derive from it. Thanks to the authority that flows from the ordained ministry, the presbyter is qualified for his office and, by divine grace, is enabled to win over people for the life lived according to the Gospel and to gather together believers into a unified community. He should bear primary responsibility and should give proof of his capacity for spiritual guidance. So the ordained minister, by his vocation, is qualified for service to the Gospel and service to man in a way that distinguishes him from others. Consequently the ecclesial ministry cannot be deduced from Christ's salvific mission to all the baptized, but only assumes a special and exemplary form in it: namely, the obligation to let "Christ be formed in them" (Gal 4:19) and hence to become an "example" for all other believers (1 Thess 1:7). "This general Christian willingness to let 'Christ be formed in them' is the necessary substratum from which the Church's ministry emerges and which is especially expressed by 'being examples to the flock' (1 Pet 5:3), as manifested in a special way by Christ. While this ministry cannot be democratically traced back to the substratum from which it comes, it nonetheless presupposes it."[7]

The roots of ministry thus understood lie in a particular investiture, which is the gift of God; human inclination and aptitude are admittedly conditions, but in the last analysis they do not suffice by themselves. If we wish to preserve the spiritual dimension of the ministry, we cannot equate this call, still less the ministerial mission, with being qualified for one of the many necessary services in the Church and in society. That ought not to lessen the value of lay professions or vocations for the community of the faithful and for humanity as a whole. But we need to draw a distinction between such professions, which can be understood perfectly well in relation to their usefulness for individuals or for everyone, and a commitment based on the grace flowing from the sacrament, which distinguishes and empowers the one ordained in a particular way.

The indications of the Bible regarding the apostolate lead to the same conclusion. They show that Christ himself founded this "office" as ministry among his first witnesses. To this ministry was assigned the particular gift of the Spirit that characterizes it and is indispensable for it. The primary task of the ministry is to bear witness to the Gospel through the priest's own life, just as Christ himself showed in an unequivocal way by the example of his life.

The vocation of priest is not realized in "immanent reasonableness" (Karl Rahner). The priest should serve his flock by following in the footsteps of Christ: serving in the manner of Christ will soon bring to light any superficial or "cut-rate"

---

[7] Hans Urs von Balthasar, 'Nachfolge und Amt,' in ibid., 80–147, here 108.

conception of ministry as seemingly reasonable as it is seductive. What alone remains valid, on the contrary, is service following Christ's example and hence a mission that does not remain something external to the messenger but seizes him to the very core of his being.

The life of Jesus and the Word of God, which according to Joseph Ratzinger's words in Pamplona form the "root cause of theology," are the indispensable criterion for the mission of God's people and of the Church's ministry. The New Testament reality, which defines this concept, at first enlists everyone who has entered into Christ's following through faith and baptism. One must hold firmly to it, with great attention and unfaltering steadfastness, for it is constantly placed in danger of being sacrificed to a self-congratulating ministerial narcissism. On the other hand, a special mission to ministerial responsibility must not for that reason be dismissed. It places its recipients firmly in the midst of the people of God as a whole, and yet is clearly distinguished by differences. Of these differences we should mention in particular: specific calling by God, proper ministerial authority for the building up of the community, and willingness and readiness to serve according to the model of the Redeemer.

2

THE PRIEST'S PERSONAL
RELATIONSHIP TO CHRIST

To let oneself be totally won over by Christ! This was the purpose of the whole life of Saint Paul to whom we have devoted our attention during the Pauline Year which is now drawing to a close; this was the goal of the entire ministry of the Holy Curé of Ars, whom we shall invoke in particular during the Year for Priests; may it also be the principal objective for each one of us. In order to be ministers at the service of the Gospel, study and a careful and continuing pastoral and theological formation is of course useful and necessary, but that "knowledge of love" which can only be learned in a "heart to heart" with Christ is even more necessary. Indeed, it is he who calls us to break the Bread of his love, to forgive sins and to guide the flock in his name. For this very reason we must never distance ourselves from the source of Love which is his Heart that was pierced on the Cross.

Only in this way will we be able to cooperate effectively in the mysterious "plan of the Father" that consists in "making Christ the Heart of the world"! This plan is brought about in history, as Jesus gradually becomes the heart of human hearts, starting with those who are called to be closest to him: priests, precisely. We are reminded of this ongoing commitment by the "priestly promises" that we made on the day of our ordination and which we renew every year, on Holy Thursday, during the Chrism Mass. Even our shortcomings, our limitations, and our weaknesses must lead us back to the Heart of Jesus. Indeed, if it is true that sinners, in contemplating him, must learn from the necessary "sorrow for sins" that leads them back to the Faith, it is even more so for holy ministers. How can we forget, in this regard, that nothing makes the Church, the Body of Christ, suffer more than the sins of her pastors, especially the sins of those who are transformed into "a thief and a robber" of the sheep (Jn 10: 1ff.), or who ensnare the Church in sin and death? Dear priests, the call to conversion and recourse to Divine Mercy also applies to us, and we must humbly address a heartfelt and ceaseless invocation to the Heart of Jesus to keep us from the terrible risk of harming those whom we are found to save.

—Homily of Benedict XVI for the inauguration of the Year for Priests
on the 150th Anniversary of the death of Saint Jean Marie Vianney,
Vatican Basilica, Friday, June 19, 2009

Incorporation in the ministerial responsibility of the Church can be established at three levels: at the level of Church activities (preaching and administration of the sacraments), at the level of canonical qualification and assumption of priestly authority, and at the level of the spiritual dimension of the action of grace. The first two of these levels are more easily accessible to empirical thought. However, the eye of faith sees in the Sacrament of Holy Orders the very foundation of the priest's identity and seeks to understand it better. When it—as Pope Benedict says with Vatican II—makes possible "action in the person of Christ," then it follows that our attention should be focused on the specific relationship to Christ that results from this sacrament.

With Christ the real *auctor ministerii* finally comes into view. The ordained minister is first and foremost a *servant* of Christ and as such is distinguished by his relationship to the Lord. It is this relationship that provides the very foundation and justification of his existence. This was formulated by Vatican II's Decree on the Ministry and Life of Priests (*Presbyterorum Ordinis*) in a series of statements that underwent revision during the process of its redaction, which lasted throughout the whole Council. The definitive empowerment by Christ, once entered into, supports each important action of the priest and creates total devotion to the Lord. So the fundamental and comprehensive requirement of the presbyter can be summed up in saying that the presbyter stands in the service (*ministerium*) of Christ, i.e., Christ is not only the model determining how the concept of "service" should be understood; Christ is also the one to whose service the presbyter is directly pledged (*genitivus objectivus*). It is Christ, again, who first makes possible the whole of the presbyter's service, when and because he makes use of the presbyter for the good of the community (*genitivus subjectivus*).

An interpretation of *ministerium* characterized above all by the ordained minister's personal relationship to God is clearly and unequivocally summed up by the keyword *service*. Undoubtedly ordained ministers are placed at the service of their fellowmen and act in their best interests; but whoever seeks the cause of this service and tries to answer the question "why," must reflect on the nature of the priest's sphere of activity. In seeking the answer, he must not let himself be preoccupied by the question of the aim or purpose of priestly action, but must turn his gaze to the *fons et origo*, the "whence" of the priest's service. In other words, he must look in quite the opposite direction: Christ alone is the root cause that supports the presbyter's sanctifying work. Being a presbyter receives its decisive quality not in the activities he performs as part of his ministry, but in the priest's subordination to Christ.

THE PRESBYTER: OFFICE AND RELATIONSHIP

But because ordained ministers also serve the members of the community, the relationship into which they enter is twofold: a relationship to Christ and a relationship to their fellowmen. This relationship can be schematized according to the threefold nature of the priest's ministry: priests as ministers of God's Word (*PO* 4); priests as Ministers of the Sacraments and the Eucharist

(*PO* 5); and priests as rulers of God's People (*PO* 6). Presbyters must therefore perform:

- *The prophetic office:* as servants of Christ in the office of prophecy, they must preach the Word of the living God, and testify to His Gospel, not their own. At the same time, as servants of man, they must prepare the way for the reception and diffusion of the message of redemption already accepted by many of their fellowmen or profoundly yearned for by others, even if only unconsciously.

- *The priestly office:* as servants of Christ in worship, they must administer the sacraments and thus make his act of redemption present anew. At the same time, as servants of the faithful, they must simply render the sign visible by preparing, not creating, the existential participation of the faithful in Christ's death.

- *The kingly office:* as representatives of Christ as Head, they must act in his name, not in their own, insofar as the mission priests perform is not theirs but Christ's. At the same time, as servants of the community, they must strive to ensure that all its members understand and embrace the personal vocation to which they have been called by God.

In the concept of being a servant of Christ the Christian view of the real contribution of the ordained minister in the process of salvation finds a perspective that gathers all his ministerial activities into one. At the same time, the priest cannot be called in any real sense a mediator; for he does not enter into the redemptive encounter between God and man as an intermediary, but assists as third person, to ensure that the encounter between the faithful and Christ takes place.

EFFECTIVENESS OF THE SALVIFIC SIGN

The priest's personal relationship to Christ is elucidated with especial clarity by the Augustinian theology of ordination. It therefore seems useful briefly to mention it. The Bishop of Hippo

(† 430) developed this theology in response to "Donatism." This North African heresy, named after its founder, the enthusiastic Bishop Donatus ("Church of Saints"), is especially important for its interpretation of the sacraments. It has its roots in the special theology of Cyprian of Carthage († 258). It will be understandable to those who recall the persecutions of the Christians during this period and the bishops' concern to protect the clergy and their communities from apostasy. According to Cyprian, a sacrament is only validly administered if the person who administers it is the bearer of the Holy Spirit, i.e., when he lives in unity with the Church; indeed Cyprian went so far as to assume that the sins of an unworthy priest would be transferred, like a physical infection, to the person who receives the sacrament from his hands. So his theology revolves around the personality of the administrator of the sacrament; all the power of salvific grace depends on the priest's holiness.

Saint Augustine attacked the heresy of Donatism: Christ, he taught, is and remains the sole bearer of the sacramental event and the guarantor of the sacrament's effectiveness. The resoluteness with which Augustine underlines the effectiveness of Christ alone, Christ unmediated, is striking. It supplies a safeguard of the ministerial action that is highly important at the pastoral level: Christ himself is at work; he remains the center and ground of hope in the individual salvific process too, so that every fearful question, every scruple, every doubt that may be aroused in the person who receives the sacrament about the holiness of the priest who administers it can be allayed.

Augustinian Christocentrism reveals the ordained ministry and the role of the presbyter in all its theological depth; it reveals the roots of the Church's ministry. These roots are too easily forgotten, with the result that the ministry instead, becomes characterized, by a utilitarian perspective: it is determined by the various tasks and activities reserved to the priest. First, Christocentrism enables us to grasp that it is not the community that creates a ministry in its midst. The ministry is not established on the basis of the generally valid experience that the continued existence of a group lacking responsible leadership is at risk. Undoubtedly the ministry is there for the sake of the community and can only be properly understood within it and on the basis of it; but in the last analysis it is legitimized neither by sociological need nor by the empowering of candidates for the priesthood, still less by the possible community election of candidates. In other words, the ministry is not established by the Church or through the Church, but must be traced back to its source in Christ himself; it is founded and rooted in him, in Christ the head of his body, the Church. Second, Christocentrism draws the ordained minister's attention to his own anchoring in Christ; the importance of this relationship both for its spiritual consequences and for the priest's understanding of his role is clear. Third, such Christocentrism warns Christians against pinning their hopes of salvation on the Church's ministers instead of on Christ himself; reflection from this perspective ought to protect many from expecting too much from the ministry and from the disenchantment to which it often gives rise. Fourth, the Christocentrism of the ministry also decisively determines the act by which someone becomes qualified for its practice. The personal relationship to Christ that is the essential prerequisite for the ministry is founded in the ordained minister soley upon the gift of grace and of the Holy Spirit, the Sacrament of Ordination itself. Ministerial action essentially needs, indeed is dependent on, a specific personal relationship of the minister himself to Christ, that is to say: his total dependence on Christ.

Being, not Action, the Foundation of the Priest's Qualification

This personal relationship to Christ is rooted in the very being of the ordained minister. It cannot be understood merely in functional or canonical or positivistic terms. The scholastic axiom that action follows from being (*agere sequitur esse*) ought not to be simply dismissed as old hat, as something incomprehensible to contemporary thought. And even if it were, the grounding of the priest's action in his personal relationship with Christ would not thereby cease. Saint Augustine also reflected profoundly on this essential premise of ministerial action.

According to this Father of the Church, legal and sociological categories cannot in the last analysis comprehend the reality of the Church. To the empirical concept of Church inculcated by the Donatists he opposed the recognition that the Church here on earth represents a mixed reality (*corpus mixtum*). For in the Church a clear distinction can be drawn between her institutional and spiritual nature: the canonically constituted institution can be differentiated from those who as community of saints and believers (*societas sanctorum atque fidelium*) form the "Church" in the real sense. Such a differentiation enables us to recognize that Saint Augustine never doubted the canonical integrity of Donatist practices. He is far from denying the validity of the sacraments of the Donatists. But these sacraments, he perceived, suffered from a crucial shortcoming: due to the rigorist theses of Donatus, the Donatists were lacking in *caritas*. And Augustine regarded God himself, ever present to us as person in the Holy Spirit, as the embodiment of this *caritas*. The canonical perfection of the Donatist system failed to give scope to this Spirit; indeed, quenched it. Augustine's theology can be formulated in this way because, in his view, the Church of the Spirit and the Church here on earth do not coincide.

The Seal ("Sphragis—Character Indelebilis")

In his theological conflict with the Donatists, Saint Augustine refuted the error which supposed an absolute mediation by the priest of the redemptive mission of the Church. In this way he ensured the Christocentrism of the ministry. To this end Augustine used theological data that he found in profane and theological history. His theological construct drew, in particular, on ideas and spiritual contents to be sought in the semantic field regarding the concept of seal (*sphragis*) as developed in the New Testament and in the Early Church. This concept expressed a number of ideas indicating that the mark imposed by a seal (*sphragis* in

Greek) is a sign of affiliation. God's spirit is their efficient force, so that "sealing" or imprinting someone with a seal should be understood as the sign of the gift of the Spirit. According to the notions of the young Church, it occured principally in the imposition of hands in baptism. In the Apostolic Fathers and in the patristic period, too, *sphragis* preeminently meant the seal of the Spirit.

The Latin equivalent of the term *sphragis* is *signaculum*. This term is found in Cyprian of Carthage to express the sign of the imposition of hands. The rite of the imposition, however, was at that time performed not only in baptism. For in the third century it was employed as a rite of reconciliation, which was also used when an apostate Christian returned to the Church. It is therefore beyond question that the imposition of hands and the rite of reconciliation were inseparably linked in the early Church. In the precedent set by the rite of reconciliation the Donatists saw a reason to demand the imposition of hands also for the rebaptism of apostate members of the Church. Augustine seems, in response to this development, to have sought a clearer term to ensure that baptism would remain a unique and once-only event: he chose the term *character* (the Greek term *character* means an indelible mark, sign, or visual device).

With the word *character*, however, Augustine seems to have particularly drawn on its specialized meaning in military language. *Character* had come to mean, in military parlance, the indelible marking of the soldier, which bound him forever to his commander. In adopting this term, the theologian refrained from any speculation about how one should conceive of the effect of baptism on the inner man; he refrained from any kind of suggestion that the spiritual event could be objectively interpreted, or even understood as a kind of brand. The Bishop of Hippo expressed himself on various occasions on the truth expressed by the theologoumenon *character*. From his many references we can deduce that a distinctive quality distinguishing and denoting the Sacrament of Baptism in the profoundest way is expressed by the visual image of *character*: the sign of being the property of the "commander" Christ, which is independent of the subjective disposition of the person who administers the sacrament and of whether he belongs to the true Church or to a heretical church.

In the present context Augustine's theology of baptism is of interest, because in elucidating the formal elements valid for baptism, he also explains the act of "ordination" and hence appointment to ministry in the Church. He thus understands ordination to the priesthood as parallel to baptism, since he does not only, or primarily, think of the sacrament as accomplishing the fullness of the effect of grace on the person who receives it. In Augustine's view, the sacraments are first of all holy signs which, especially in the case of baptism and ordination, should be understood as "markings": characters indelibly imprinted on one who receives them. For both these sacraments have their foundation in consecration, in an act that creates a specific and permanent relationship between God and man. So, according to Saint Augustine, ordination, too, following the model of baptism, should be regarded as a once-only sacrament that indelibly marks the ordained person and remains in him (character).

This mark of belonging to God, precisely because it is indelible, can also become a kind of mark of Cain (cf. Gen 4:15): Augustine himself conjectures a possible unholy outcome bound up with the sign when he says that it will bring "the wicked to judgment." The indestructible relationship to God that is marked with a sign is, however, above all a help that no one should do without. For Augustine, the reason for the "permanence" of the character-marked Sacrament of Ordination lies in God's trust. This trust had been preserved in the finality of the priesthood of Jesus; it is manifested in his salvific mission to man and in his covenant. So the character can really be regarded as the indestructible pledge of the promise of God. But that does not mean it should be taken for granted. As Pope Benedict XVI exhorted all the ordained during the Chrism Mass in Saint Peter's in Rome on April 13, 2006, the friendship

with Christ imparted by the sacramental sign of the imposition of hands needs to be rediscovered each day. It "sums up an
entire existential process." It is something to which the priest
must daily recommit himself: the ordained "should know Jesus
in an increasingly personal way, listening to him, living together
with him, staying with him."

The "What" of Character

At a later period in the history of the Church the idea of the
indelibility of the "character" often led to its objective misunderstanding. For Saint Thomas Aquinas it was still a "sign," but
no longer was it a mark of external identification. Instead, in his
Aristotelian-scholastic conceptual system, the "character" was an
interior sign: it marked man from within in a far-reaching way. It
expressed the concept of being configured to Christ that was not
exhausted in mere presence. It had as its aim the priest's designation for divine worship (*deputatio ad cultum divinum*). With this
designation the "character" could develop its own unequivocal
meaning: the seal of salvation conferred during baptism can be
distinguished from the act of ordination that designates someone
for divine worship.

The great interest aroused by the "what" of character and
its more intensive ontological development led to a growing
separation between the notion of configuration to Christ and
that of designation for divine worship. This led the way, in the
fourteenth century, to the erroneous interpretation of "character" as a "fixed and immovable quality" (J. Galot). Luther's
repudiation of this interpretation led to a further step in the
reification of character. At the Council of Trent the conciliar
Fathers wanted to hold firm to its reality and to whatever
was necessary to rebut Luther's error; this led to an isolated
and unilateral emphasis (DH 1774). Thereafter, in the period
before the Second Vatican Council, important dogmatic manu-
als, though recognizing the centrality of "character," made little
effort to focus attention on the meaning of the concept. The

equating of character with ordination then obscured the theologically and existentially fundamental personal relationship to
Christ, and yet it was precisely this that had shown the way
to the spiritual reality of ordination which the broadening of
Augustinian thought helped to elucidate.

Even more disastrous was the fact that the above-mentioned
identification of ordination with the mark of "character" failed
to address the real basis of presbyteral action, the specific gift of
the Spirit. This opened the way to a new error: character was no
longer understood as a mere sign that refers to the priest's being
configured to Christ. Instead of the dynamic that it necessarily
had to develop as part of its nature, the static nature of its presence was emphasized. The Ordo no longer had any finality, any
ultimate goal; it seemed to be there for its own sake alone.

Although the insights of an earlier era, based on a "reified
ontology," cannot simply be dismissed, today it is necessary as
much as possible to express what has so far been said of "character" in the categories of personalism—though without in any way
incurring the suspicion of modern simplification. Reality is indeed
thought of today as man-based; anthropocentric ideas help us to
gain a better understanding and also serve—if applicable—to
win acceptance for doctrinal truths. We ought therefore to find
a mode of expression for "character" that simultaneously keeps
in focus its spirituality and its symbolic sense bound up with
the action of man. In this perspective, a significant element of
character grows from the conscious and affirmative fulfillment
of ordination: "character" is the consequence of a decision. This
subjective decision is raised by the sacramental rite to such an
intellectual and spiritual level that it acquires lasting validity in
the subjective and ecclesial spheres.

A RECENTLY DISCOVERED SERMON
OF SAINT AUGUSTINE

Saint Augustine treated the truth of the personal relationship of the ordained minister to Christ in a sermon of which an excerpt is here published for the first time in English translation.[1] That even after an interval of over 1500 years texts are still being discovered of this great Father of the Church, whose theological insights are so pregnant in so many fields, is not just a curiosity. His words in this sermon provide us with an authoritative synthesis of ideas I have attempted briefly to express above.

"At this point," says Saint Augustine in this sermon, "I am reminded of something that is very painful for me to mention, namely, the fact that Parmenianus, a former bishop of the Donatists, dared to maintain in one of his letters that the bishop was the mediator between the people and God. So you see that they [the Donatist bishops] themselves sit in the place of the Bridegroom. With blasphemous adultery they corrupt the souls of others. This arrogance is no small matter. Indeed it seemed to me wholly incredible, had I not read of it with my own eyes. For if the bishop were the mediator between the people and God, a consequence of that would be—since there are so many bishops—that one would have to imagine a multitude of mediators. So, to subscribe to the letter of Parmenianus would be tantamount to destroying the letter of the apostle Paul, who says: *For there is one God, and there is one mediator between God and*

---

[1] In 1990 François Dolbeau, Professor at the École Pratique des Hautes Études in Paris, while doing research in the Stadtbibliothek in Mainz, discovered in a fifteenth-century manuscript in the library's collection (shelf mark I 9) 26 sermons of Augustine that hitherto had been unknown to modern historical research. Sermon No. 26, an excerpt of which is being published here, was given, according to Dolbeau, in Carthage on January 1 in the year 404; it is especially devoted to the pagan New Year's customs, the false theology of the Donatists, namely that the priest was the intermediary between God and man, and the one true mediation of Christ through his once-only sacrifice on the Cross.

A German translation of the sermon does not yet exist. But it is expected that one will be published in 2009, in the series "Patrologia," Vol. 22, Frankfurt: Peter Lang Verlag.

men, the man Christ Jesus (1 Tim 2:5). But between whom does the mediator stand if not between God and his people? In other words, between God and his body, since his body is the Church. That arrogance is therefore fathomless that dares to install the bishop as mediator by claiming, with adulterous deceit, Christ's bond of betrothal for himself.

"Let us contemplate instead the friend of the Bridegroom, who rejoices in the Bridegroom, and does not place himself in the Bridegroom's place. Does he say: 'I have myself betrothed you to me'? Only he who calls himself mediator between people and God can say such a thing, not he who says: *Was Paul crucified for you? Or were you baptized in the name of Paul?* (1 Cor 1:13); nor he who says: *For there is one God, and there is one mediator between God and men, the man Christ Jesus* (1 Tim 2:5); nor he who says: *I betrothed you to Christ to present you as a pure bride to her one husband* (2 Cor 11:2). Therefore, he who possessed no wedding garment and was cast out of the wedding hall is an adulterer [cf. Mt 22:1–14]. For he did not possess the garment in which he ought to have honored the Bridegroom. Instead, he strove through his own outward appearance to advance his own honor at the marriage feast of the Bridegroom (no. 52).

"So, brethren, for us there is only one mediator, who is also our Head. As for us, even if we differ from you in being placed as leaders of the Church, we are nonetheless members of the [one] Body of Christ together with you in Christ's name. We have one head, not many. For a body that wants to have many heads is definitely a monster.

"As for the anointing, however, we said that formerly only priests and the king were anointed, but now all Christians are anointed. So from this it can be grasped that all of you together with us belong to the body of the [one] priesthood, because all of you are believers. The fact that those who govern the Church are designated in a special way with the name of priests does not mean that the other members of the body are not part of the [same] priestly body.

"That is why in those arcane rites of antiquity only one priest entered the Holy of Holies, because in these rites only one was prefigured, namely he who is also called our Lord and Priest Jesus Christ, while all the people however remained standing outside. But now that the bishops stand at the altar, are you perhaps still left standing outside? Don't you enter inside to see and hear? Are you not witnesses and recipients? In former times the one priest entered the Holy of Holies only once each year. One year stood for time as a whole. So, once in time as a whole, our one Priest, who rose from the dead, the Lord Jesus Christ, who offered himself as a sacrifice for us, entered the Holy of Holies, no longer in a figurative way, but in truth, on the other side of the curtain of heaven. He entered into it, and there he remains. But the people still remain standing with us outside. We have not yet risen to go toward Christ and remain with him forever in the inner [sanctum], if he be pleased to say to the good servant: *Enter into the joy of your master* (Mt 25:21, 23).

"So, at that time, what was intended by the one priest, who alone entered the Holy of Holies, and the people, who remained standing outside, was what came to pass through our Lord Jesus Christ, who alone entered into the mysteries of heaven, while the people still sigh outside, but have been saved in hope and await the redemption of their body, which lies in the future resurrection of the dead. Nonetheless we have one Priest and High Priest who enters into the Holy of Holies for us, and who sits at the right hand of the Father. So, during our pilgrimage here [on earth] we don't need to live in fear, so long as we don't stray from the way of truth and don't love another instead of him, but mutually love each other in him, so that in each of our brothers who goes on Christ's way, we may recognize him, honor him, and accept him *who was put to death for our trespasses and raised for our justification* (Rom 4:25). For he himself speaks in his saints, as the apostle says: *Since you desire proof that Christ is speaking in me* (2 Cor 13:3).

"And although he says: *So neither he who plants nor he who waters is anything, but only God who gives the growth* (1 Cor 3:7), he says so because he wished that not he himself, but that God should be loved in him. That is why he confirms some as follows: *You did not scorn or despise me, but received me as an angel of God, as Christ Jesus* (Gal 4:14). So, he himself, is to be loved in all his saints, because he says: *I was hungry and you gave me food, I was thirsty and you gave drink* (Mt 25:35). For he does not say: 'You have given to them,' but *'You have given to me.'* So great is the love of the Head for his body" (no. 53).

3

THE SPECIFIC GIFT
OF THE SPIRIT

Our pilgrimage to the holy city would not be possible if it were not made in the Church, the seed and the prefiguration of the heavenly Jerusalem. *Unless the Lord builds the house, those who build it labor in vain* (Ps 126:1). Who is this Lord, if not our Lord Jesus Christ? It is he who founded his Church and built it on rock, on the faith of the apostle Peter. In the words of Saint Augustine, *It is Jesus Christ our Lord who himself builds his temple. Many indeed labor to build, yet unless the Lord intervenes to build, in vain do the builders labor* (Enarratio in Psalmos 126:2).

Dear friends, Augustine goes on to ask how we can know who these builders are, and his answer is this: *All those who preach God's word in the Church, all who are ministers of God's divine Sacraments. All of us run, all of us work, all of us build,* yet it is God alone who, within us, *builds, exhorts, and inspires awe; who opens our understanding and guides our minds to faith.* What marvels surround our work in the service of God's word! We are instruments of the Holy Spirit; God is so humble that he uses us to spread his word. We become his voice, once we have listened carefully to the word coming from his mouth. We place his words on our lips in order to bring it into the world. He accepts the offering of our prayer and through it he communicates himself to everyone we meet. Truly, as Paul tells the Ephesians, *he has blessed us in Christ with every spiritual blessing* (1:3), for he has chosen us to be his witnesses to the ends of the earth, and he made us his elect, even before we came into existence, by a mysterious gift of his grace.

—*Pope Benedict XVI, Celebration of Vespers with Priests,*
Members of Religious Orders, Seminarians, and Deacons
in Notre-Dame Cathedral, Paris, September 12, 2008

Vatican II's Decree on the Ministry and Life of Priests (*Presbyterorum Ordinis*) went through seven (!) different preliminary drafts. Their contents were in part rejected, in part modified, and increasingly accepted in the Council's individual sessions. It was not until November 1965 that the decree was finally put to a vote and the text adopted.

In the final phase of the decree's redaction some conciliar Fathers had attacked what they called the "legalism" of the version: this, they claimed, had unduly influenced its formulation. In fact the section of the Constitution on the Church *Lumen Gentium* more specifically referring to priests (*LG* no. 28), which had been adopted by the Council a year earlier and so does not reflect the complete conciliar *aggiornamento*, does not contain any explicit reference to the Holy Spirit and his irreplaceable participation in the Sacrament of Ordination. Some bishops therefore complained of what they perceived as the text's undue subservience to Western legalistic thought and lack of theological depth. These objections thus led to the clear formulation of the final redaction: "Hence the priesthood of priests, while presupposing the sacraments of initiation, is nevertheless conferred by its own particular sacrament. Through that sacrament priests, by the anointing of the Holy Spirit, are signed with a special character and so are configured to Christ the priest in such a way that they are able to act in the person of Christ the head." (*PO* no. 2; cf. *LG* 11). Vatican II thus confirmed the Orders as a sacrament, as indeed the Council of Florence (1439) had already done.[1]

---

[1] Cf. W. Breuning, *Communio Christi. Zur Einheit von Christologie und Ekklesiologie.* Düsseldorf, 1980, 246–250.

The reference to the gift of the Holy Spirit and its transmission by the imposition of hands has been corroborated anew by more recent biblical studies as a practice in the early Christian Church. According to these studies, what is described in the Second Letter of Paul to Timothy (1:6) as "rekindling the gift of God that is within you through the laying on of my hands" is an act by which the ministry in the Church is founded. The effect of this imposition has been described as "sacramental"—and rightly so, thanks to a further theological advance.[2] For what it imparts is the gift of the Spirit. This is expressed in a variety of ordination formularies and forms the center of the act of ordination. These texts, including their liturgical instructions, need to be consulted for a proper understanding of the ordination of priests. This corresponds to the ancient ecclesiastical conviction that theological truth has an important source in liturgical prayer (*lex orandi—lex credendi*).

LITURGY OF ORDINATION

Let us begin with *The Apostolic Tradition* (*Traditio apostolica*), which is regarded as the oldest consecration formulary that has come down to us. It remained valid in the early Church for several centuries. It goes back to Hippolytus of Rome († 235). According to this treatise, in which Hippolytus describes the various spiritual gifts that "God, right from the beginning, granted to people according to his will," the rite of ordination of ministers essentially takes place through the laying on of hands and the prayer of consecration.

If we take ordination as bishop as the model of the ordination rite, as Hippolytus expressly proposes, the laying on of hands is at first performed in silence after the invocation to God: "He who is ordained as a bishop, being chosen by all the people, must be

---

[2] During the final editing of the present study Cardinal Walter Kasper has published, in a collected edition, the investigations he has devoted to the ordained ministry in the Church over the last four decades: *Die Kirche und ihre Ämter* (Freiburg, 2009). Justice cannot be adequately done to this magnificent book here. Certain divergences from the publication I am offering here will not of course escape the discerning people.

irreproachable. When his name is announced and approved, the people will gather on the Lord's Day with the council of elders and the bishops who are present. With the assent of all, the bishops will place their hands upon him, with the council of elders standing by, quietly. Everyone will keep silent, praying in their hearts for the descent of the Spirit. After this, one of the bishops present, at the request of all, shall lay his hand upon him who is being ordained bishop, and pray" (no. 2).[3] The prayers of ordination for all other clerics in the *Traditio apostolica* agree with this model, in which the Spirit is conferred by the imposition of hands.

The prayer that follows the laying on of hands invokes the gift of the Spirit: "Look upon your servant here, and impart the spirit and wisdom of elders (*presbyterium*), that he may help and guide your people with a pure heart, just as you looked upon your chosen people and commanded Moses to choose elders, whom you filled with your spirit which you gave to your servant" (no. 7).

The imparting of the spirit of grace and of the wisdom of the council of elders (*presbyterium*) forms the crux of the prayer. It forms the central act of consecration. It is further exemplified and underlined by the Old Testament model of the conferral of the spirit on Moses and the seventy elders (Num 11:16–25). This imparting of the Spirit, which causes a close and enduring bond of attachment to God and the capacity for wise judgment, undoubtedly is directed to the helping and guiding service that the ordained minister offers to the People of God, but it is not directly aimed at satisfying the needs of particular and specifiable individual activities.

Admission into the *presbyterium* seems to be the essential social effect of ordination. That is remarked by the *Traditio*'s rubrics on the ordination process, when it is said of the presbyters present at the rite that they alongside the bishop shall also lay their hand on the ordinands. The gift of the Spirit as

---

[3] See *The Treatise on the Apostolic Tradition of Saint Hippolytus of Rome, Bishop and Martyr.* London: Alban Press, 1992. An English translation of the *Traditio apostolica* is also available online: *www.bombaxo.com/hippolitus.html.*

the presbyter's distinguishing feature is unmistakably expressed in this. For in the accompanying instruction we read: "The presbyters place their hands because of a common spirit and similar duty." That this conferral of the Spirit must constitute something specific to the priest can be inferred from the rubric on the consecration of deacons (no. 8). For there it is stated that the deacon "does not receive the spirit" that qualifies the presbyter. So the gift of the Spirit specified in the *Traditio apostolica* is clearly conceived as distinguishable from that of another degree of ordination, and the consecration for each degree of ordination transmits the particular gift that is characteristic of it. What differentiates the individual presbyter from non-presbyters connects him specifically with the presbyteral college, so that such a college can be regarded as "the place where this Spirit reigns."

GREEK FATHERS OF THE CHURCH AND ORTHODOX FORMULARIES

More markedly than in the Roman tradition, the Eastern Church sees the gift of the Spirit as the center and decisive point of ordination. This is confirmed by several Greek Fathers of the Church, who trace back the apostolic mission and service to the sending down of the Spirit. They recognize this connection in the rite of the baptism of Jesus in the river Jordan: "And when Jesus was baptized, he went up immediately from the water, and behold, the heavens were opened, and he saw the Spirit of God descending on him" (Mt 3:16; Mk 1:10; Lk 3:21–22; Jn 1:32–34). The filling of the Lord with the divine *pneuma* they also interpret as the spur, the motivation for the consecrated person to lead a life devoted to the Gospel. In their theological conception the qualification and sending out of the apostles was thus realized on the Day of Pentecost, when the Holy Spirit descended on them "like the rush of a mighty wind" (Acts 2:2), following the model of the descent of the Holy Spirit on Jesus.

The martyr Saint Irenaeus of Lyon († 202) thus teaches that the Holy Spirit descended on the young community at Pentecost as it had done on Jesus himself following his baptism in the river Jordan; "for he has power over all peoples, to lead them into life and to open up the New Covenant to them." Athanasius († 373) meditated on Psalm 133: "it is like the precious oil upon the head, running down upon the beard, upon the beard of Aaron." So the anointing of the Holy Spirit is first conferred on the Head of the Church, namely, Christ himself, then on the beard, symbol of the apostles, who are the adornment of the face of the Church. That happened in Jerusalem, and through the apostles all the faithful have received the eternal blessing. According to John Chrysostom († 407) Jesus received the anointing of the Spirit in the Jordan; it was granted to the Twelve at Pentecost; in this way they were also empowered to transmit the Holy Spirit to others. Lastly, Cyril of Alexandria († 444) drew the same parallel between the descent of the Spirit on Jesus at the Jordan and the gift of the Spirit to the apostles at Pentecost: "Just as the voice of the Father made itself heard from heaven and gave witness for his own Son with the words 'This is my beloved Son, with whom I am well pleased' (Mt 3:17), so God gives a clearer sign of his grace by sending down tongues as of fire also on the apostles."

The spoken invocation of the Holy Spirit is also found in several characteristic ordination formularies of the Orthodox Church. The texts invoke the filling "with the Holy Spirit, with grace and with good counsel"; they call for "the gift of the Spirit," for election through "the presence of the Holy Spirit," and for illumination and the transmission of the light that is the Holy Spirit. An essential plea of the Orthodox Church to the Churches of the West is, indeed, that the meaning of the Holy Spirit be "discovered anew" (P. Evdokimov): it is clear that such a plea is quite specifically relevant to the scope and importance that the Holy Spirit ought to have in the understanding and theology of ministry.

RIGHT AND WRONG QUESTIONS

Whoever grasps that the particular mission of ordained ministers rests on the gift of the Spirit will no longer limit himself to a sociological or functional account of the priest's identity. The question posed in the title of this book "Why Priests?" is not pointless: it has its sense, but it cannot hope to comprehend the essence of the consecrated priesthood and the empowerment of service that ordination confers. The many concrete activities in which the presbyter's consecrated authority is expressed cannot be listed as it were in a catalogue, as if all his various roles could be itemized in a kind of job description. Still less can the individual elements that make up the Church's mission be bundled together in a differentiated canonical system. At what pastoral tasks should the authority (*potestas*) that ordination confers be aimed? Or in what services for the building up of the community could the presbyter dispense with an empowering, sacramental *potestas*? Which of them does he believe he can master by his own unaided natural talents without the aid of the grace that was conferred on him by his ordination?

It is therefore impossible for various reasons to wish to define what is specific to the presbyter, and what differentiates him from the non-ordained, by attempting as it were to compile a catalogue of his special qualifications, in order to demonstrate in this way the necessity or rationale of ordained ministers in the Church. "One asks oneself, therefore, what the priest really is, why he still exists today, when on the one hand almost everything that he himself possesses in terms of special authority, and almost everything he does, can be done just as well by others. [. . .] But if one asks such questions, and if one dissects and analyzes the task of the ministerial priesthood in all its individual parts in the style of the usual school theology, one finds, in the end, that the question has been posed in the wrong way."[4]

---

[4] Karl Rahner, 'Theologische Reflexionen zum Priesterbild von heute und morgen,' in *Schriften zur Theologie* IX. Einsiedeln, 1970, 380f.

4

"ORDINATION AND MISSION" AS KEY TO UNDERSTANDING

Dear brother priests, let us ask the Lord Jesus for the grace to learn for ourselves something of the pastoral plan of Saint Jean Marie Vianney! The first thing we need to learn is the complete identification of the man with his ministry. In Jesus, person and mission tend to coincide: all Christ's saving activity was, and is, an expression of his "filial consciousness" which from all eternity stands before the Father in an attitude of loving submission to his will. In a humble yet genuine way, every priest must aim for a similar identification. Certainly this is not to forget that the efficacy of the ministry is independent of the holiness of the minister; but neither can we overlook the extraordinary fruitfulness of the encounter between the ministry's objective holiness and the subjective holiness of the minister.

—*Pope Benedict XVI, Letter Proclaiming a Year for Priests, June 16, 2009*

A LOOPHOLE IN REFLECTION?

According to the doctrine of the Church a ministry exists on the basis of which someone can act in the person of Christ. So the question is inevitably posed how such action can be made possible. The ability to act in this manner cannot be assumed without further ado and on the basis of indeterminate grounds. Anyone conscious of the unique importance of Jesus Christ for our salvation cannot fail to qualify action on his behalf as important, indeed, momentous, and its character of being extraordinary arises in the first instance from the fact that such action exists at all. It must also characterize the perception of the person who acts as Christ's representative: in view of the responsibility he is about to assume, surely no one would dare to lay claim to such a ministry on the basis of his own entitlement. For the natural gifts that someone brings with him for this kind of ministerial service are clearly insufficient. Whoever wishes to make the Lord present in his action can do so only by drawing on the power of Christ himself.

Unfortunately, the bishops assembled from all over the world for Vatican II paid scant attention to Orders, understood as sacrament. Clearly practical presbyteral service interested them more than sacramental and spiritual empowerment. This service, however, demands a reflection not only on the theological locus of the presbyter in the Church and on the coherence of his functions, but also on the empowering grace that makes his action possible in the first place. The dogmatic core of the Sacrament of Holy Orders, in which the service assumed by the presbyter and the self-understanding of its bearer are anchored, at first emerged only slowly in the conciliar discussion. Clearly this logic was something of which the Council Fathers themselves became increasingly aware. Conceptual progress in the theology of ministry, as it came to be formulated first in the Constitution of the Church, and then in the Decree on the Ministry and Life of Priests, was thus gradual: during the conciliar debate it emerged ever more clearly that participation in the priesthood of Christ constitutes the core of the priest's mission; that the sacramental event of ordination transmits this core; and that, through it, the candidate is configured to the image of Christ the Head and is enabled to act in his person.

Although valuable, however, these insights were too abstract to have much catechetical force; mere footnote citations frequently referred to decisions made, or resolutions adopted, at the Council of Trent. In the development of trains of thought, they tended to remain wedded to pragmatic arguments, without reflecting on the systematic theological grounding of their own statements. Mere affirmations predominated. That is particularly to be lamented in terms of reflection on what actually takes place in the sacramental ordination itself. For this shortcoming sometimes led in post-conciliar discussion to the problematic consequence of skimming over the theological and existential basis of the priest's existence as "unimportant theory" and preferring instead speculative new conceptions. As a counter-tendency it is therefore worth attempting to elucidate the implicit idea of ordination that animated the Council Fathers. Formulations and traces in the Decree on the Ministry and Life of Priests (*Presbyterorum Ordinis*)—whether intentional or not—will help us to grasp it.

JESUS AS MODEL

The few times that the term "ordination" (*consecratio*) is used in *PO* is itself revealing for the significance that should be attached to the Sacrament of Holy Orders. In the text of the decree the term is used for the empowering and constitutive induction of ordinands into presbyteral service: configured to Christ, "they are consecrated to God in a new way in their ordination" (no. 12).

It might seem worthwhile, in this connection, to enquire into the early Christian use of the term *consecratio*, in order to gain insights into the Council's conception of *Ordo*. Yet, in truth, the theology of the Church Fathers proves to be of little help. It confirms a striking diffidence about, even a refusal to expound, the use of the term. The early Church clearly was averse to explaining Christian Revelation with expressions culled from the religious terminology of pagan Rome (such as *consecratio*), for it professed and taught that with the sacrifice of Christ all pagan cult practices had been dismissed as idolatry. It was not until a later period, once the Church had acquired freedom of worship and misunderstandings were less to be feared, that the term *consecratio* became more generally accepted and used in the Church. The Decree on the Ministry and Life of Priests therefore does well to read the concept "ordination—*consecratio*" in the biblical context and in this way to avoid making misleading pronouncements in terms of religious history and cult practice.

The text of the decree in no. 12 understands the substantive *ordination* as synonymous with the verb used by the Evangelist John to mean "sanctify" or "consecrate" (*hagiazein*; Jn 10:36: those "whom the Father hath sanctified, and sent into the world," as it is translated in the King James Bible, those "whom the Father consecrated and sent into the world," in the Revised Standard, and Jerusalem Bibles). With this term the decree introduces the example of Jesus into its interpretation of the act of ordination and enriches it with new and deeper content in the light of the history of salvation: "Christ, whom the Father sanctified or consecrated and sent into the world, 'gave himself for us to redeem us from all iniquity and to purify for himself a people of his own who are zealous for good deeds' (Tit 2:14), and in this way through his passion entered into his glory. In a similar way, priests, who are consecrated by the anointing of the Holy Spirit and sent by Christ, mortify the works of the flesh in themselves and dedicate themselves to the service of the people, and so are able, in the holiness with which they have been enriched in Christ, to make progress towards the perfect man" (no. 12).

Clearly a concept of sanctification deduced from the redemptive mission of Jesus has an incarnated structure. Reflecting its origins in the pagan history of religion and in the Old Testament, it means something similar to the concept of consecration derived from the pagan sphere; the cultic background of "consecration" consequently can never be denied. But the cultic and sacral origins of the term, while reflecting its traditional connotation, can only be a "means of sanctification" at the New Testament level. Its assignment to a particular sphere—here that of ordination— ought not for a Christian to stray into a trivializing idea, as if pagan scope or a heathen context were to be postulated with it;

rather, it should be understood as transcending time and place and having a spiritual connection.

Still further corrections to a spontaneous understanding of "sanctify" can be made through an exegetical study of the use of the term in the New Testament. They lead to something decidedly other and to a slightly forgotten connotation of the term. According to the Evangelist John, the process of sanctification does not mean any separation from the "world" or passing over to a place that "belongs only to God." Jesus' sanctification, indeed, takes place precisely because he had been sent *into* the world. He is the one "whom the Father consecrated [sanctified] and sent into the world" (Jn 10:36).

CONCEPTUAL PAIR AS HERMENUETIC TOOL

According to Rudolf Bultmann, the two verbs *consacrare* (*hagiazein*) and *inviare* (*pempein*) express the same thing through the rhetorical figure of doubling. This insight is illuminating. It grasps the inseparable unity between consecration and mission (*missio*/sending forth). The two terms cannot be divided into two consecutive acts. The verb *consacrare* is used in the active in the Prayer of Jesus: "...I have sent them into the world" (Jn 17:19). The verse explains that consecration does not, nor can it, mean advancement to any special dignity. For at the beginning of the narrative of the Passion that immediately follows the Prayer of Jesus (in John 18), it becomes clear that consecration is consummated in the sacrifice of one's own life; it consists in Jesus' active and voluntary abandonment to death. The New Testament significance of consecration here coincides with that of service (*ministerium*) as defined by Jesus and discussed above.[1] If we wish to regard the presbyter's initiation as central in this, we ought to call the sacrament not only ordination but also *consecratio*, consecration; for the term expresses more clearly God's

---

[1] See Chapter 2, "The Priest's Personal Relationship to Christ."

total taking possession of the presbyter, which is realized in total dedication to his fellowmen.

That consecration and mission mean two aspects of the one and the same reality was clearly something of which the Council Fathers were aware: in the text of the decree, consecration is thrice immediately followed by a reference to *missio*. The repeated juxtaposition of *missio* with consecration and the application of this conceptual pair to the ordained priest brings home to us that "mission" not only involves every baptized person in the Church, but also contributes something important to the proper understanding of the Church's ministry.

Someone who bears in mind the decree's statements on *ordination* and places them in the context of mission will be convinced of the great value of the conceptual pair *consecratio et missio* for our understanding of ordination. Both words, in their reciprocity, point in the first place to their Johannine origin. At the same time, the juxtaposition of the two terms and their application provide the basis for an interpretation in the New Testament setting crucial to our understanding of priest. This context corrects the more restrictive meaning that can arise from an interpretation drawing only on the history of religion (pagan use of *consecratio*) and the Old Testament. In the last analysis it is Jesus' exemplary act of redemption alone that establishes the sense of this conceptual pair. In the act of consecration we become "instruments of service."[2]

One apparently negative consequence, however, follows from this: namely, that consecration, if it has its model in the New Testament model of service and if service leads the consecrated person in turn to an attitude of self-abandonment, does not elevate one to privilege or "reverence." Still less can the "being sent forth" denoted by this word pair qualify the presbyter for ministerial action in any special way: it is not "sending forth," it is not *missio*, that differentiates him from the "merely baptized"; for

---

[2] Pope Benedict XVI, Homily at the Chrism Mass in Saint Peter's Basilica, April 13, 2006.

mission is a duty of *all* members of the people of God. Beyond this delimitation, however, the word pair *consacrare* and *inviare* (consecration and mission) can also help positively to clarify the act of initiation to the presbyter's service. This positive interpretation is all the more convincing the more closely the two points of reference of this conceptual pair coincide and the more inseparably connected they are seen to be: on the one hand, the model of consecration, Jesus himself, who provides the norm, and, on the other, the Sacrament of Baptism as an exemplary parallel of ordination.

In the light of these reflections, the significance of the Sacrament of Ordination can now be better understood:

1. It comes to man from outside his self. Though it requires his freely given assent, it is not in the last analysis the result of his own planning or of his own freely taken decision.

2. It is God-given: God is its agent, its cause: neither human assent nor social circumstances fundamentally support and guarantee its reality.

3. It claims the whole person. It not only makes possible the fulfillment of particular functions or qualifies its recipient for a particular professional role, but more importantly engages him in a close personal bond.

4. It tolerates no limitation, neither the posing of conditions to limit the readiness for service depending on subjective choices and circumstances, nor any limitation in time. Rather, what stands behind it is a fundamental claim/demand on its recipient, which takes effect once and for all and involves every member of the People of God and all our fellowmen. That is why it must be expressed in practice in total dedication— even if the fulfillment of this duty can never satisfy the ideal.

Thus the word pair *consecration* and *mission* can be regarded in some sense as the key concepts enabling us to grasp the Sacrament of Ordination. Yet neither of these terms, nor even both together, in any sense coincide with the concept of ordination—as if they were synonymous with the word *ordinatio*. It seems more suitable, together with Edward Schillebeeckx and Heinrich Schlier, to underline the fact that the concept of "consecration" is indispensable in the presbyter's initiation.

CREDIBILITY OF MISSION
AND OBLIGATION OF CELIBACY

The scripturally founded conceptual pair *consecration* and *mission* provides the basis for the spiritual claim made upon ordained ministers, if only we read into it God's total taking possession of them and their total dedication to mankind. The ordained minister in the Church is indeed exposed to particular spiritual and ascetic demands. Are these demands justified, are they legitimate, even assuming that Augustine was right in his theological argument against the Donatists, namely, that the effect of the sacramental salvific sign is independent of the ministrant's worthiness?[3]

Karl Rahner adduced convincing arguments to show that the Church needs holy priests. He started from the premise that (as Augustine taught) though the effectiveness of the sacrament does not depend on whether the priest who administers it is a man of true faith, nevertheless only ministers sustained by a life of faith and charity can in the long run guarantee "the existence and permanence of the sacraments as a whole in the Church." For the priest's word will only be credible, will only be accepted in good faith by the person listening to him, if his will is prepared and his inner ear opened. The priest's credibility is therefore essential. The person who is given full authority to administer the sacramental Word of God to his fellowmen has, according to Rahner, "also the right and duty to produce the context for the proclamation of the faith in which alone these sacramental words find the 'disposition' or 'situation' in which they can be pronounced at all and listened to with faith, and in which they are really capable of

---

[3] On Saint Augustine's anti-Donatist argument, see above, 33–36.

being translated into reality."[4] That means that a specific obligation to live the Word of God in a credible way is intimately bound up and necessarily grows from the ministerial task to serve the preaching of the Gospel. If the Church must also be a motivation for faith, then the presbyter as the person who is given the task of serving all the faithful has an even heavier responsibility to bear. Therefore his spiritual action as a priest cannot only have its cause and mainspring in the fact of being Christian.

Apart from referring the faithful to the Gospel of Jesus, the various attitudes and practices of the presbyter should especially be aimed at strengthening his personal attachment to Christ, his friendship with him. "You belong to me," says Christ in words put into his mouth by Pope Benedict: "At the center [of the Sacrament of Holy Orders] is the very ancient rite of the imposition of hands, with which he [Jesus] took possession of me, saying to me: 'You belong to me.'"[5]

Instead of attempting a catalogue of the various obligations and duties of the priesthood, however, here it is my intention only to focus on one obligation, that of celibacy, the unmarried state for those who are "consecrated" and "sent forth." The candidate for ordination feels its enormous claims on him in a particularly radical way. Of course, it is only a canonical obligation, a law of the Church that could as such be amended. In some cases, even within the Church, it is found objectionable; it is seen as an imposition that burdens priests in an even more crippling way. Yet what do such objections say against its significance?

"He who is able to receive this, let him receive it" (Mt 19:12): this is the lapidary comment made by our Lord himself to the question posed about celibacy "for the sake of the kingdom of heaven." Clearly, therefore, even in Jesus' time, the meaning of this form of life was obscure; it was difficult to grasp. And how even less convenient, how even more difficult to grasp, is

---

[4] Karl Rahner, *Kirche und Sakramente*. Freiburg 2nd edn., 1960, 91.
[5] Benedict XVI, Homily at the Chrism Mass in Saint Peter's Basilica, April 13, 2006.

"celibacy for the sake of the kingdom of heaven" today! It conflicts all too blatantly with contemporary lifestyles, not only
because long overdue doctrinal pronouncements have restored to
matrimony the rank and dignity of its biblical understanding, but
also because everything worldly holds us so much in thrall that
we want instant gratification. Continence as a virtue has been
discredited: the proverb "a bird in the hand is worth two in the
bush" holds good for us all.

Despite that, ecclesial realism cannot annul the sentence
about celibacy for the sake of the kingdom of heaven. The
meaning of celibacy will of course remain obscure, so long as
"the wisdom of the wise, and the cleverness of the clever" (1 Cor
1:18ff.) hold sway. But it cannot be deflected, still less refuted,
with worldly logic.

Consecratio and *missio* unavoidably lead, according to the measure of Jesus, to total self-immolation on the cross; but in it God's
love is revealed in a definitive way. All charity in the Church only
succeeds, therefore, if it be the reflection of the divine love that
takes the form of oblation. The eucharistic love between Christ
and Church remains committed to the form of the *memoria
passionis*, the memory of Christ's suffering.

In such a perspective the celibacy that the Church demands
of the priest is the eschatological sign *par excellence*. It did not
grow from sexual inhibition. It was not prompted by sexual
disgust. It is not a legacy of Platonism or spiritualism. Rather,
Jesus, with his birth to the Virgin Mary, with his celibate life,
with his death and Resurrection, brought a new value, indeed a
new dimension, to love. Sexual reproduction received a certain
"theological insignificance" (Hans Urs von Balthasar) from the
history of salvation. Christianity is about being reborn to a new
life: "Celibacy is a sign of this new life to the service of which
the Church's minister is consecrated; accepted with a joyous heart
celibacy radiantly proclaims the Reign of God" (*Catechism of the
Catholic Church* 1579). According to the martyr Bishop Irenaeus
of Lyon († *c.*202), the fruitfulness of the Virgin Mary is at one

with the fruitfulness of the Virgin Church (*Adv. haer.* IV, 33, 4). It is therefore appropriate that those who ministerially represent the Church should represent the Virgin Birth, existentially, as well. Celibacy does not mean hostility to the body: it means that the incarnation of the Word of God from the Virgin stands at the very dawn of our faith.

With his remarks on the difficulty of comprehending this celibate life, Jesus allows us to perceive that the mystery is only dispelled in a new horizon of understanding, the horizon of faith.

1. Celibacy permits a greater availability of the priest for service in the community. In addition, it can become a visible exhortation to a fulfillment of man that has yet to take place. Whoever experiences this exhortation in his life will testify thereby to a significant aspect of the Gospel. Celibacy is therefore appropriate for those in the Church who are given the task of proclaiming the Gospel of eternal life. One who understands how to interpret this reference will be strengthened in the same hope that the Gospel brings with it, and will lose the fear that the happiness he longs for in the here and now will forever be denied to him.

2. Celibacy as an obligation is a challenge for the man who embraces the priesthood. He has to recognize that neither worldly values nor his fellowmen can give him security for the dangerous path on which he has embarked. He can only assume such a risk if God supports him. So the hurdle of the law, the canonical prescription, poses the crucial existential question whether he really believes in God in the active Father Jesus Christ in his life—or whether God is for him only a figment, an "imaginary God" (Meister Eckehart).

Celibacy has in it something of the "folly of the cross" (1 Cor 1). Indeed it only acquires its full sense when the multitude fail to comprehend it: "For the foolishness of God is wiser than men, and the weakness of God is stronger than men" (1 Cor 1:25). However, if no more believers were to be found in our communities who could see an important meaning in celibacy, then in the long run priests would no longer be able to support this obligation: they would break under its burden; even the sociology of knowledge recognizes that any conviction we hold must inevitably collapse if it is no longer supported by any of our fellowmen. What Jesus says about the difficulty of understanding this celibate life is therefore at the same time an exhortation constantly to rediscover the meaning of celibacy in the community of faith.

A LAMENT OF SAINT THÉRÈSE OF THE CHILD JESUS

Consecration and mission are the roots of holiness and as such an opportunity for the priest. But they give him no guarantee of holiness. One of the convent letters written by the young Saint Thérèse of the Child Jesus (1873–97) contains the telling words: "How many bad priests there are, how many priests who aren't holy enough! We pray, we suffer for them . . . , do you understand the cry of my heart?"

Of course, the reader will ask himself just what the gentle Saint, whose vocation was love, might have meant here: practitioners of simony, hoarders of sinecures, hunters after benefices? Men of no faith? Ambitious power-hungry careerists? Perhaps. Above all, however, she meant those priests who, as Hölderlin put it, "practice the divine like a trade," those whose nature is cold and indifferent, men without spirituality.

II

❧

DEVELOPMENTS

5

COMMUNIO IN
THE PRESBYTERIUM

This communion of priests is more than ever important today. In order not to drift into isolation, into loneliness with its sorrows, it is important for us to meet one another regularly. It will be the task of the diocese to establish how best to organize meetings for priests—today we have cars which make travelling easier—so that we can experience being together ever anew, learn from one another, mutually correct and help one another, cheer one another and comfort one another, so that in this communion of the presbyterate, together with the bishop we can carry out our service to the local Church. Precisely: no priest is a priest on his own; we are a presbyterate and it is only in this communion with the bishop that each one can carry out his service. Now, this beautiful communion, recognized by all at the theological level, must also be expressed in practice in the ways identified by the local Church, and it must be extended because no bishop is a bishop on his own but only a bishop in the college, in the great communion of bishops. This is the communion we should always strive for. And I think it is a particularly beautiful aspect of Catholicism: through the primacy, which is not an absolute monarchy but a service of communion, that we may have the certainty of this unity. Thus in a large community with many voices, all together we make the great music of faith ring out in this world.

—*Pope Benedict XVI Meeting with the Clergy of the Diocese*
of Bolzano-Bressanone, August 6, 2008

FELLOW-HELPERS OF THE BISHOP

Though it was the bishop who transmitted the qualifying gift of the Spirit through his laying on of hands in the Sacrament of Ordination, he is not its ultimate cause. For the act of administering the sacrament, in spite of its "lasting effect," is not something that transcends the constraints of time, but is limited to the dimension of man and history. The bishop may facilitate the presbyter's encounter with Christ through the liturgical action, but his role is limited; it remains confined to the space of the serving sign that Christ communicates through him. Rightly understood, therefore, no minister of the sacrament appears once and for all as mediator in Christ's place. Any tendency to identify grace and office in the Church or to consider "the Church as ministerial source of grace," is therefore erroneous. Cyprian of Carthage († 258) had identified the Old Testament high priest, without reference to Christ, as the prototype of the bishop; his error paved the way to the Donatist heresy.

So, though the episcopal ministry has an essentially referential character, by referring the presbyter to Christ, it also has a particular task of watching over the diocese: in particular, the bishop must guard against any self-centered isolation of parishes within his local church and ensure that the local church is not inward-looking but kept open to the worldwide communion of the Church. Whether the unity of faith of the universal Church is preserved and celebrated in the plurality of forms essentially depends on the bishop. And presbyters assist him in fulfilling this obligation.

In the Acts of the Apostles Luke, in describing Paul's dramatic departure from Miletus (20:18–35), summed up what then and now must be said to all ordained ministers, both to the presbyters who came from Ephesus (v. 17) and to the bishops (v. 28). Together they have the task—his imperative is plural—to tend the flock of which "the Holy Spirit has made you guardians" and "to feed the church of the Lord" (v. 28). They are doubly armed for this task: through the Holy Spirit and in their responsibility to preserve "the whole counsel of God" (v. 26f.). They do so col-legially, for example, in combating heresy.

During Vatican Council II the Fathers did not go into the complicated question of the origins of the ministry of bishops and priests in the early Church. They simply tried, in accordance with their pastoral concerns, to establish the Ordo of bishops as a model for the Ordo of priests. They call presbyters "fellow-helpers" (*cooperatores*; PO 8). The term, however, is ill-adapted to the theological difference between these two degrees of ordination. Indeed, almost the same sacramental authority is accorded to the presbyter as to the bishop (cf. PO 7). On the other hand, if we think of the reciprocity between episcopal and presbyteral activ-ity at the canonical level, we find that, while the service of the presbyterate is comparable to that of the bishop, it is also defined by canonical dependence on the latter. That goes for all three fields of endeavor of the priest's mission: teaching (PO 4), liturgy (PO 5), and the power of ruling over God's people (PO 6). The decree expresses the conferral of these basic offices on presbyters with the term "*missio canonica*" (canonical mission: PO 7).

POST-APOSTOLIC ROOTS

In elucidating the relationship of the bishop with the presbyter, we should not therefore lose sight of its two fundamental aspects: the canonical subordination of priest to bishop on the one hand, and their "common sharing of the same priesthood and mission" and "spirit of cooperation" (PO 7) on the other. The sacramen-tal aspect of the relationship can be best explained in terms of the concept and reality of an institution in the early Church, the *presbyterium* (council of elders). It therefore seems useful to examine this institution in some detail, both because it throws light on the basic "common sharing of the same priesthood and mission" of ordained ministers, as established by the Sacrament of Ordination and because it is helpful for an accurate idea of the *presbyterium* or council of priests.

The letters of Saint Ignatius of Antioch († before 135) contain no less than thirteen references to the ecclesial communion among the ordained. In a text we have already mentioned, the *Traditio Apostolica* of Hippolytus of Rome († 235), the liturgical function of the *presbyterium* is explicitly expressed: it receives a separate mention, alongside the community of the faithful, in the choice of bishop. The *presbyterium* plays no active role in the consecration of the bishop ("With the assent of all, the bishops will place their hands upon him, with the council of elders standing by": no. 2). By contrast, the members of the *presbyterium* do play an active role in the ordination of new presbyters: they lay their hands on the ordinands after the bishop "because of a common spirit and similar duty" on the part of the clergy (no. 8).

From the letters of Pope Cornelius († 253) and Bishop Cyprian of Carthage, lastly, we can infer that the *presbyterium* participated in the government of the Church. Thus Cyprian stresses that he had made it his rule to undertake nothing without the advice of the presbyters, and Cornelius assembled the *presbyterium* in Rome to decide on how to proceed with the supporters of Novatian—who lived around 250—and to end the schism.

Thereafter, however, the unity of the *presbyterium* became loosened in the course of the history of the Church. Already during the persecution by the emperor Decius († 251) Cyprian gave the members of the *presbyterium* permission to celebrate the Eucharist with a deacon taken in rotating order from the ranks of the diaconate. The Synod of Sardica (343) prohibited the establishment of an episcopal see wherever a single presbyter sufficed. Towards the end of the fourth century a development began that attempted to limit the presbyters' subordination to the bishop. The close bond between the *presbyterium* and the bishop was thus weakened, and the role of the bishop as *primus inter pares* correspondingly reinforced. The priest's understanding of his own ministry was ever less founded on the bishop. It was not until Vatican II that the theological reality of the presbyterate was placed in a new light. It could be supported not only on a well-confirmed patristic practice, but even more instructive for our own time is its theological foundation in the early Church. Both for bishops and priests it lies in the common Spirit they received in the sacrament of the Ordo, which establishes a specific community between both levels of the hierarchy, namely *communio*. With this important *theologoumenon* another reality comes into view which had great strength of character in early Christianity and was powerfully revived in the Second Vatican Council. Its roots lie in the celebration of the eucharistic sacrifice.

THE MEANING OF THE TERM
COMMUNIO HIERARCHICA

The eucharistic event, according to early Christian testimonies, should be regarded as "sign and *causa efficiens* of the ecclesial community ..., more precisely as *causa efficiens* of incorporation in the community."[1] Again and again, and with particular emphasis, the martyr Bishop Ignatius († before 135) points to the necessity of the unity of the Christian community and the growth and reinforcement of this unity through the celebration of the Eucharist, for instance in his Epistle to the Philadelphians: "Take heed, then, to have but one Eucharist. For there is one flesh of our Lord Jesus Christ, and one cup to [show forth] the unity of his blood; one altar; as there is one bishop, along with the presbyters and deacons, my fellow-servants" (Chapter 4).

The reciprocity between Eucharist and *communio* can also be inferred from the practice of excommunication. This disciplinary measure in the Church shows that in the early days of Christianity participation in the celebration of the Eucharist and the reception of the Lord's Body were considered the root cause of *communio*; for exclusion from the community and readmission to it found their most reliable expression respectively in the refusal

---

[1] G. Hertling, '*Communio* und Primat—Kirche und Papsttum in der christlichen Antike,' in *Una Sancta* 17 (1962) 91–125, here 98.

of the Eucharist and the excommunicated person's readmission to the sacraments, while the shattering of *communio* with the bishop was expressed by forbidding people to attend Mass and receive the Eucharist from his hand.

A second important factor that can help us reach an understanding of the term *communio* is that *communio* is not a reality that can be produced by man: it is a supernatural *donnée* that is granted to man by gift of the Spirit. Nevertheless it is regarded as something real, something that exists, something that is independent of the will or thought of the individual person. This understanding can to some extent appeal to the Pauline motif of the Body of Christ (cf. 1 Cor 12). On the other hand, it contradicts many modern and contemporary ideas of unity, which only take into consideration the human contribution to the existence of each community and would therefore like to derive *communio* from a human association among its members into which they freely enter.

Yet *communio* is before man, and is not created by man. This rules out any kind of association established for a particular purpose as a model for understanding its reality. Neither solidarity of support in the time of the persecution of Christians, nor the special interest groups aimed at ensuring the continued existence and growth of the Church, can help us explain this *theologumenon*. "What bound together the individual bishops in unity in Antiquity was not the conviction that they had perforce to stick together in order to *achieve something*, but the conviction that this unity is present, as a state, independent of what the individual feels or thinks or does." So G. Hertling formulates, perhaps a bit too aphoristically, the "objectivity" of *communio*.

Communio: *Antecedent, Binding, and Liturgically Renewed*

It is understandable that *communio*'s precedence as a state that is preordained, imposes certain conditions on those who want to participate in it: they are asked to offer themselves to an already existing reality and to incorporate themselves in it. The fact that *communio* is distinguished not only by a sacramental, but also by a juridical bond then becomes clear. It corresponds, namely, not to some vague, non-binding community feeling, but is ordered, i.e., reveals itself as "confessionally bound," and in it the individual is subordinated to a discipline that also intervenes in the private sphere. The binding nature of the conditions for admission gives to the idea of *communio* an indispensable juridical character, according to which someone will be refused communion at the level of the local church if he is excluded from the communion of another church. Yet the fact that this canonical connection is characterized and supported by a sacramental root should in no case be minimized; the concept of *communio* can indeed emphasize that the canonical aspects do not spring from positivistic caprice, but are a development from the sacramental reality that is grounded in the faith.

The belief in an antecedent unity that is beyond or outside human effort, that comprehends the concept of *communio*, and that effectively describes the eucharistic meal and bread, became a formative element of the idea of the Church during the first millennium. It was especially given form in Saint Augustine's "ecclesiology." Peter Lombard († 1160) had still not forgotten this idea of *communio* and its residual Augustinian coloring in the twelfth century.[2]

Another medieval theologian, Gerhoh von Reichersberg († 1169) was also influenced by Augustinian theology when he wrote: "The whole of Christ is turned into food in the sacrament celebrated on the altar; but he who consumes it does not transform it into part of himself, in other words, as nutriment for his flesh; but rather he himself is transformed in Christ, so that he may become a member of his Body, which is the one Church, redeemed and nourished by the one Body of Christ."[3]

---

[2] Cf. Henri de Lubac, *Corpus mysticum—Ein Symbol kirchlicher Einheit und sein Nachleben im Mittelalter.* Einsiedeln, 1969, especially 215–228. Strictly speaking Augustine developed no ecclesiology, but "ecclesiological" aspects flow from his teachings on the Eucharist as source of *communio*.

[3] Cited in ibid., 221f.

The idea of *communio* also finds expression in the liturgy and more particularly in the custom for individual parishes to exchange particles of the eucharistic Host, the Body of the Lord, in order to represent and by the consumption of the one bread, to become the unity of Christ's Body. The bishops testified to their *communio* among one another by sharing the Host. This practice helped to bring together local churches that were sometimes geographically far apart; it was continued down to the Synod of Laodicea (second half of the fourth century). The connection with the local bishop and within the diocese was later expressed and created with the help of *fermentum*: namely, the practice of carrying a particle of the eucharistic bread—perceived as the leaven of Christian life—from the bishop of one diocese to the bishop of another; the receiving bishop would then consume the Species at his next celebration of the Eucharist as a sign of the communion between the churches. In Rome itself the custom seems still to have been in use in the ninth century. While its symbolism, according to one eleventh-century witness, later seems to have been scarcely understood in general in the celebration of the Eucharist, there are indications in German, Spanish, Roman, and French pontificals that this practice was still continued as late as the fourteenth century in the case of the consecration of bishops and that the meaning of the *fermentum* was still understood.

Undoubtedly the submission of the presbyter to the bishop, as required by canon law, should not be infringed. Vatican II's Decree on the Ministry and Life of Priests was formulated by men who had no doubt come across a recalcitrant and rebellious spirit in their dealings with their presbyters. They therefore insisted: "Priests for their part should keep in mind the fullness of the sacrament of Order which bishops enjoy and should reverence in their persons the authority of Christ the supreme pastor. They should therefore be attached to their bishop with sincere charity and obedience" (no. 7). That notwithstanding, the relationship to the bishop always remains comprehended within the merciful dependence of both bishops and priests on the High Priest Christ. There is one ministry, whose service is made possible by the one gift of the Spirit and to which they are called by the one sacrament. It is not only their common sharing of the same faith in Christ that brings together priest and bishop, but also a specific brotherhood, which the common Ordo establishes. Such communion between them takes precedence over all differentiations and defines them in a crucial way. It will place the relationship between bishop and priest in the light of the faith also in situations of tension. It neither emphasizes authority nor insists on the law, but listens to "what the Spirit is saying to the churches" (Rev 2:7, etc.).

So, in the light of the above, the following aspects should be emphasized with regard to *communio* in its application to the Sacrament of Holy Orders:

1. Christ's Gospel provides the fundamental norms for the preaching of the Good News. Political or media power may occasionally exert influence that is damaging to the faith and to members of the Church who call themselves Catholic. But such influence is no part of "*communio*" of any kind. For *communio* tolerates no compromise, no adjustment of the Word of God to the fashions of the day. The truth of the faith, which always transcends and takes precedence over any human interpretation, empowers and obliges the Church's ministers to resist any kind of distortion or falsification of the truth; this can be taken to the point of open resistance, such as that of Paul's resistance to Cephas: "I opposed him to his face" (Gal 2:11).

2. Christ's life and death are the ever valid example to be followed. It is in the personal encounter with Jesus that spiritual action acquires its significance. His existence and his life are alone able to leave their mark on a credible messenger of his Gospel. Church circles can themselves dictate a functional or utilitarian mentality and 'fixation on structures'; Jesus' life

teaches us not to conform to them. Sociological status, like scientific and cultural expertise, should on the contrary be subordinated to the overriding pastoral need.

3. It is Christ's Spirit that makes pastoral service possible. The presbyter is in reality the collaborator of the bishop and not just his executive organ. New approaches to pastoral ministry and pastoral initiatives require the bishop's approval, but are often a sign of renewal and more a sign of the power of the Spirit actively at work in our time than the stale monotony of routine. The relationship to the bishop alone cannot explain the presbyter's personal lack of success or the deep misunderstandings he sometimes experiences. The obligation to obey the promptings of the Holy Spirit keeps the priest in an attitude of service, while his readiness to listen to the bishop's words makes his own action fruitful.

Communio Hierarchica: *A Well-Ordered Relationship*

The essentially Christocentric interpretation of *communio* must hold good as a fundamental datum for understanding ministry in the Church. Yet it would be paradoxical if, in the attempt to trace the origins of the notion of *communio*, we were to remain confined to the individualizing aspects. The fundamental individual and personal relationship to Christ indissolubly parallels the communion between bishop and priest and provides its foundation. The adjective *hierarchica*, hitherto left unconsidered, is crucial for the wider understanding of this relationship.

In the documents of Vatican II the term *communio* is often supplemented with this adjective (*communio hierarchica*). It is admittedly alien to the early Christian terminology in this connection and hence linguistically not particularly happy, but, in the light of our short excursus on the history of the term, it is revealed in substance as an articulation of the binding canonical structure of the Church in the sense of a wholly sacramentally anchored law. "*Communio*," as the then Cardinal Ratzinger taught, "is an expression for the sacramentally determined canonical structure of the early Church and indicates the original reason and connection of the Church's canonical conception [...]. The canonical building up of the Church is performed in the canonical communion of, and inter-communication between, the episcopally governed *ecclesiae,* also in a hierarchical communion of sacramental content—this precisely is the sense of the phrase *hierarchica communio,* which should show to advantage the early ecclesial concept of *communio* as clearly as possible as the fundamental canonical and existential form of the Church for all time and also for today."[4]

From the theological meaning of the concept of *communio* the following conclusion can be drawn: the relationship in question is supported by a profound communion between bishop and presbyter. *Communio* in this sense is the expression of the *one* ministry, whose service is empowered by the one gift of the Spirit and to which ministers are called by the one sacrament. Recourse to the adjective *hierarchica* during the Council was intended to dispel any concern lest the concept of *communio* could in some way obscure, or weaken, the binding character of the sacramentally anchored canonical structure of the Church. The addendum, however, unfortunately reinforced the tendency for the emphasis to be displaced, from the sacramental to the canonical structure, and for the expression of the communion of ordained ministers to be no longer formulated via the interpretation of the concept of *communio hierarchica* as a whole. Instead, one started out from the term *hierarchica* and concerned oneself either primarily or exclusively with the clarification and delimitation of canonical responsibilities.

There is no doubt that today administration, bureaucracy, and structural reform are gradually leading to a shift in perspective, from the category of grace to that of law, even in sociological thought. Misguided application is made of political methods or

---

[4]Joseph Ratzinger, 'Kommentar zur *Nota explicativa praevia* der Kirchenkonstitution des Vaticanum II,' in *Das Zweite Vatikanische Konzil. Kommentare, Dekrete und Erläuterungen.* Teil I, Freiburg, 1966, 353.

social practices to processes within the Church. It is no longer the spirit of *communio* but power politics that determine feelings and decisions. The models of communion in the Church are left in the lurch. These models are transmitted by the Bible—fathers and sons, brothers and sisters, friends and companions; a deeply human dimension is intrinsic to them all and takes precedence over any legalistic dimension. And the consequence is that the Church hardens on its various levels into a system perhaps more functionally efficient but cold. Especially the bishop's relationship to his priests is here put to the test. Vatican II's Decree on the Ministry and Life of Priests insists on the need for brotherhood between bishops and priests: "On account of this common sharing in the same priesthood and ministry then, bishops are to regard their priests as brothers and friends" (*PO* 7).

With this declaration an inner boundary of the ecclesial and social relevance of the concept of *communio* becomes visible: the sacramental gift of the Spirit is something that its recipient owes in the last analysis not to particular men, but to Christ himself. Nor can it be reduced to ecclesial and social relationships, which are not its cause but its consequence. So the relationship that is forged in the Ordo is preeminently a specific relationship to Christ, transcending every tangible expression in the relationship between bishop and presbyter and everything deducible from it. The presbyter is therefore distinguished more by an individual relationship to, or rather communion with, the Lord himself than by anything else. In the Lord the priest recognizes his dependence on the bishop. Therefore an exclusively canonical conception of the ministerial reality would not only remove the presbyter from his raison d'être, Christ himself, but would include him in the bishop's canonical competence in such a way as to jeopardize the aspect of *communio* as source of divine grace.

COUNCIL OF PRIESTS

Thus rooted in the practice of the early Church, the meaning of the term *presbyterium*, which Vatican II placed in a new light, becomes clear. According to the Code of Canon Law of 1983, it is further represented in the council of priests within each diocese (canons 495–502): "In each diocese," says canon 495, "there is to be established a council of priests, that is, a group of priests who represent the *presbyterium* and who are to be, as it were, the bishop's senate." To this council are assigned a number of advisory tasks to support the bishop in the governance of the diocese, "so that the pastoral welfare of that portion of the people of God entrusted to the bishop may be most effectively promoted" (ibid.). These tasks are individually defined and organized according to the requirements of diocesan law. However indispensable clear forms for the communion between bishop and his *presbyterium* are for the mission of the Church, the spiritual reality of the *presbyterium* cannot be reduced to compliance with *canones*. It would be a lamentable impoverishment were the *presbyterium* to be shrunken to mere compliance with canonical prescriptions that regulate the respective roles of a bishop and his priests. The fact that it is necessary to refer to canon law at all is in itself a measure of the danger to which the spirit of *communio* is exposed.

A particularly moving witness of the early Church was Bishop Ignatius of Antioch († 107). It is possible that he had, as a young man, even met the apostles Peter and Paul, whose writings were normative for him. Under the emperor Trajan († 117) he was condemned to a martyr's death by being thrown to wild animals. He yearned profoundly to be ground into God's wheat: "Allow me to become food for the wild beasts. I am the wheat of God, and let me be ground by the teeth of the wild beasts, that I may be found the pure bread of Christ."[5] He fervently implored the Romans to do nothing to save or reprieve him: "For if you are silent concerning me, I shall become God's; but if you show your

---

[5] Saint Ignatius of Antioch, *Epistle to the Romans*, Chapter 4.

love to my flesh, I shall again have to run my race. Pray, then, do not seek to confer any greater favor upon me than that I be sacrificed to God [...]."[6]

But this urge for martyrdom in order finally to attain to God and be a "true man" in Christ, does not make him forget tirelessly to call for concord and harmony among the communities. Concord is possible from the common spirit of the *presbyterium*. The unity of servants flowing from the hierarchy is to him the source of the unity of the community within itself and with God: "For there is one flesh of our Lord Jesus Christ, and one cup to [show forth] the unity of his blood; one altar; as there is one bishop, along with the presbytery and deacons, my fellow-servants."[7] So Pope Benedict XVI recurs to the normative tradition of the early Church when he emphasizes (as he did in his meeting with the clergy of the diocese of Bolzano-Bressanone) the brotherly communion between bishop and presbyterate, the "*communio affectiva et effectiva*," as the great strength of the Catholic Church.

---

[6] Ibid., Chapter 2.

[7] Saint Ignatius of Antioch, *Epistle to the Philadelphians*, Chapter 4.

CONSCIOUS
AND LIVING FAITH
ON THE SPIRITUALITY OF PRIESTS

And yet the burdens have increased. To be looking after two, three, or four parishes at the same time, in addition to all the new tasks that have emerged, can lead to discouragement. Often I ask myself, or rather each of us asks himself and his brethren: How are we going to cope? Is this not a profession that consumes us, that no longer brings us joy since we see that whatever we do is never enough? We are overburdened!

What response can be given? Obviously I cannot offer infallible remedies: nevertheless I wish to suggest some basic guidelines. I take the first one from the Letter to the Philippians (cf. 2, 5–8), where Saint Paul says to all, especially of course those who work in God's field: "Have in yourselves the mind of Christ Jesus." His mind was thus that, faced with the destiny of humanity, he could hardly bear to remain in glory, but had to stoop down and do the incredible, take upon himself the utter poverty of a human life even to the point of suffering on the Cross. This is the mind of Jesus Christ: feeling impelled to bring to humanity the light of the Father, to help us by forming the kingdom of God with us and in us. And the mind of Jesus Christ also deeply roots him in all-pervading communion with the Father. An external indication of this, as it were, is that the Evangelists repeatedly recount that he withdraws to the mountain alone, to pray. His activity flows from this profound union with the Father, and precisely because of this, he has to go out and visit all the towns and villages proclaiming the Kingdom of God, announcing that it is present in our midst. He has to inaugurate the Kingdom among us so that, through us, it can transform the world; he has to ensure that God's will is done on earth as it is in heaven and that heaven comes down upon earth. These two aspects belong to the mind of Christ Jesus. On the one hand we must know God from within, know Christ from within, and be with him; only in this way will we discover the "treasure." On the other hand we must also go out towards others. We cannot simply keep the "treasure" to ourselves; we must hand it on.

—*Pope Benedict XVI, Address at the Meeting with Priests and Permanent Deacons, Saint Mary's Cathedral, Freising, September 14, 2006*

SPIRITUALITY IN SOCIAL RESEARCH

Empirical social research primarily rests on quantifiable data and findings accessible to statistical analysis. The life of the spirit, by contrast, is not susceptible to such treatment: it cannot be analyzed, for example, from the enumeration of spiritual exercises or from the individual demands of spiritual action. So spirituality cannot easily be measured by a questionnaire or sociological survey. Interpretation must try, instead, to recognize and explain the spiritual forces that inspire a person to live according to God's will, and try to throw light on a person's general outlook or point of view that has motivational importance for his intentions and decisions. Spirituality, in other words, is expressed in the reactions that the content of revelation arouses in the spiritual attitude of the person attuned to it. It is therefore only deducible indirectly and in complex measurements, especially because the data that determine human will and action are, by their very nature, largely unsusceptible to statistical surveys.

Described as "the subjective side of dogmatics,"[1] the spiritual life is like the window through which the whole of the revelation

---

[1] Hans Urs von Balthasar, 'Spiritualität,' in: *Verbum caro.* Einsiedeln, 1960, 226–244, here 227.

is interpreted and converted into life. The reflections that follow are offered in this light: they are aimed at elucidating the tangible and demonstrable stages of human action and penetrating, where possible, to the motivational forces that inspire them.

Ever since the beginning of the history of the Church the "spirituality of the Church as *sponsa verbi*" (Hans Urs von Balthasar) has been distinguished by man's changing horizon of faith, the circumstances of his life and his shifting motives. The demanding call of the Gospel penetrates into man's specific living conditions, into the contingencies of his daily life: in other words, the Christian will make particular decisions by seeking in the circumstances of his daily life for impulses of faith rooted in "ultimate truths" [*Letzteinsichten*]. So when he is able to discover a valid Gospel message in the contingencies of time and place, or when an exemplary figure or inspiring model appears on his horizon, then the voice of spiritual life is heard.

It takes the form of a call, impelling man to make a fresh start. This impetus propels man to discover not only interior values but also religious truths. For faith is quickened, and its truth illuminated, from the circumstances of his daily life. At the same time, man's physical nature has as its consequence that, as a general rule, immanent motives more strongly influence his conduct and attitude: personal bonds, social and political involvement, cultural interests, and recreational activities speak directly to him. Not least, man's human environment and profession leave their mark on him. The same undoubtedly is true also for priests. Work and leisure activities also influence their spiritual life—just as, vice versa, their spirituality should have a reflex influence on their daily routine.

Given the countless variety of individual devotional exercises, we can conclude that spirituality is a force that transcends its individual forms: it is "the habitual coordination of the conduct of man's life by his *ultimate truths* and *fundamental decisions*."[2] Through

---

[2] Hans Urs von Balthasar, 'Das Evangelium als Norm und Kritk aller Spiritalität in der Kirche,' in idem, *Spiritus Creator*. Einsiedeln, 1967, 247–263, here 247.

spirituality all the baptized, and not least all ordained ministers, are rooted in a basic datum, the decision to follow God. So spirituality tries in the last analysis to use the various means necessary to tap into God's relevance for the fulfillment of human life.

GOD'S RELEVANCE AS "ULTIMATE TRUTH"

Opinion polls on priests have hardly been conducted in the German-speaking countries in recent years. The latest data we have at our disposal are those of the survey conducted by the *Arbeitsstelle für kirchliche Sozialforschung* (agency for Church-based social research) in Vienna.[3] They have been evaluated on the basis of four selected types of how the ministry of priests is understood.[4] In the questionnaire itself the data that concern our present theme are only touched on briefly[5] and are limited to mentioning traditional factors as spiritual aids: prayer books, Sacrament of Penance, spiritual exercises, eucharistic adoration, individual and group reflection, daily pastoral service. So the questionnaire did not inquire into the fundamental motivations of priests or the faith on which their spirituality is based. No attempt was made to inquire into the roots of spirituality and ascertain through questions what is empirically comprehensible. Yet it is only through such an inquiry that one would be able to penetrate to the "ultimate truths" of priests' life of faith.

---

[3] Edited by P.M. Zulehner as "Forschungsbericht der Studie" (= FB) "Priester 2000" (Ostfildern 2001); cf. also the summary "findings" (= E) of this report under the title *"Sie gehen und werden nicht matt." Priester in heutiger Kultur*, eds. P.M. Zulehner and A. Hennersperger, Ostfildern 2nd edition 2001. The Catholic pastoral theologian Paul Zulehner, who had published an uninterrupted stream of studies in the field of the processing of statistical data on the Church and undoubtedly has a thorough and reliable overview of the situation, maintains that no larger-scale inquiries on the life and service of priests have been carried out in Europe since 1971 (E 13). Wholly without any interest in priests seems to be the recently conducted "Sinus-Milieu" study conducted on behalf of the German Bishops' Conference Sinus-Milieustudie: *Hinaus ins Weite. Gehversuche einer milieusensiblen Kirche*, eds. M. N. Ebertz and H.-G. Hunstig, Würzburg n.d.; despite the theme of "Church" in its title, no references at all to priests will be found in this publication.

[4] Cf. the second of the publications cited in the previous note.

[5] Only 15 of the 450 pages are devoted to spiritual life in FB.

This superficiality must be pointed out, especially since we are dealing here with a pastoral-theological survey, not with a secular sociological inquiry conducted by some kind of professional group or polling agency. The limitation is all the more surprising since the survey report itself touches *en passant* on the crux of the success or failure of the priest's existence. The report's "theses on the situation of the Church" thus admit: "The main cause for this pessimism (of priests) lies in the cultural crisis of faith that J.B. Metz calls 'crisis of God'" (FB 39).

Unfortunately, the dimension of faith cannot simply be taken for granted in regard to the service and life of priests. While the proposition that "pastoral care sanctifies the pastor" is true, it has to be admitted that faith can atrophy; it can wither away. Faith is not *eo ipso* conferred. On the other hand, the service of the ordained minister can become torture if the heart rebels against it or if the faith that inspires it is no longer there. The relationship to God thus has crucial importance for the human willingness of the ordained minister to perform the mission to which he is called.

The question is of supreme importance: How does faith impact on the service and life of priests, what effects does it have on them? Has it perhaps become dulled in the secularized environment of our time? No one who wants to help the presbyter to a fulfilled life can push this problem to one side; not least, because it is of such high relevance for the individual and for the Church in the extremely painful process that leads a priest to abandon his ministry.

Cumulative data compiled by the Congregation for the Clergy report 1,754 applications for abandonment of the priesthood and return to lay state in the years from 2006 to 2008. The bare figures don't begin to suggest the inner struggles, the heartbreak and discontent, the conflict with fellow Christians that many priests suffer, or the troubles and confusion that the loss of their vocation causes in the communities to whose pastoral service they are assigned.

The return to lay state is, after due examination, occasionally granted, but the step is not taken lightly. Anyone who carefully studies the reasons cited by the applicants will be surprised to find that scarcely any of them situates the starting point for their turning away from the clerical vocation in spiritual life and devotional practice. So, for instance, one priest writes: "Clerical duties and the priest's way of life were a matter of indifference to me." Another writes: "I asked myself: What is already definitive in this world? So I didn't bother about praying, and the sacrament of Penance and only celebrated Mass when required to do so." A third explains that it was only the money that still interested him. "I no longer had any time left for prayer and for study of the Word of God in order to prepare my homily. I loved gambling. The consecrated life no longer had anything to say to me." One priest told me, long before presenting his application for a return to the lay state: "I only pray during Mass, because that is the service I am required to perform for my fellowmen." Yet experts familiar with many applications for return to lay life declare that the turning away of priests from the ministry began in 90% of cases with the loss of personal faith, the cooling of their personal relationship with God.

A Past Statistic for a Present Problem

An opinion poll that aims to discover something about the priest's personal relationship to God is difficult to conceptualize; perhaps that is why no attempt has been made to conduct one in recent years. However, due to the impact this relationship has on the life and service of priests, the approach ought not to be abandoned. At the same time, it seems highly desirable that any such survey should be based on hard data; for hard facts generally are more persuasive.

Fortunately, as part of the bishops' synod in the Federal Republic of Germany, an extremely differentiated survey of the clergy was conducted, also on behalf of the German bishops' Conference, in the early 1970s. The questionnaire priests were asked to complete consisted of 96 questions, some of them heavily sub-divided. Of the over 26,000 questionnaires sent out, 20,131 were returned, the 76% return rate ensuring a reliable sample. The evaluation of the data was assigned to G. Schmidtchen, Professor of Social Psychology and Sociology at the University of Zurich, who published his findings in 1973. They show that the survey questionnaire was not limited to the more superficial aspects of priesthood, but also penetrated into the deeper motivations of the priest's vocation, its grounding in personal faith.[6]

The Priest's Ministerial Obligation to Bear Witness

The fact that spirituality is bound up with daily life is undoubt-edly something that priests and laity have in common. The spirituality of all Christians is identical in formal terms, insofar as one is called to take seriously and fulfill the "service" that goes with it. The life of priests and laity is characterized by the fact that both groups have a role to play in relation to their fellow-men and the world.

However, the norm of daily duties cannot be the only guide-line. The Christian is convinced that his life has a higher dimen-sion; it is not exclusively aimed at achieving earthly goals. The world is for him at the same time God's creation, and he believes that all forms of this creation are assigned a higher meaning in God's plan. So the question of meaning inevitably points him beyond worldly values. God and his Word come into view for him as a new horizon and a new source of motivation. This is what qualifies the Christian's service and is at the same time the source of its integration. It is this inner core of personal faith that prevents various forms of spiritual action from disintegrating into conflicting forms of spirituality. Only the impulse that is derived from the Word of God and tries to follow in its spirit deserves to be called "spirituality" in Christian life.

---

[6] *Priester in Deutschland. Forschungsbericht über die im Auftrag der Deutschen Bischofskon-ferenz durchgeführte Umfrage unter Welt—und Ordenspriestern in der Bundesrepublik Deutschland.* Freiburg, 1973; cited below as FBP.

Every form of spirituality that can claim to be Christian must show this theocentric dynamic. There is a second reason why such theocentrism is required for the spirituality of the priesthood: namely, his specific "service" as an ordained minister in the Church. For this service is predicated not, as in the case of the laity, on the pursuit of a secular profession, but on the preaching of the Gospel. Ordained ministers have to bear the heavier burden of responsibility arising from the fact that the Church not only has to speak the Word of God, but must also inspire faith. The presbyter's spiritual action is thus aimed not only at fulfilling the tenets of his own Christian faith, but also at meeting a specific obligation peculiar to him and flowing from his ordination.

A simplified but telling correspondence with this specific duty of ordained ministers was reflected in another opinion poll, conducted among all Catholics in Germany.[7] In reply to a question about the "essential tasks of the priest today" (FBS Table A 68) a task described as "giving an example through his life" received a middling importance with 46% of the respondents checking this particular box; it was considered more important than the priest's involvement in ecclesial groups (43%), educational work (36%), or political activities (10%).

That priests themselves also bring a particular sense of spiritual obligation to their work as priests is apparent also in another connection. Here another question in this opinion poll, about the most important means for the promotion of new vocations to the priesthood, deserves attention. Out of sixteen proposals for improving the situation, "more spiritual liveliness in church" received the fifth largest percentage in terms of boxes checked; and in more recent years this percentage increases, pushing this option into fourth or even third place (FBP Table A 66).

Responses to the question whether, and for what, there was still any free time for other things apart from priestly activity

---

[7] G. Schmidtchen, *Zwischen Kirche und Gesellschaft. Forschungsbericht über die Umfragen zur Gemeinsamen Synode der Bistümer in der Bundesrepublik Deutschland.* Freiburg, 1972; cited below as FBS.

suggest the importance that priests would like to attach to prayer, meditation, and spiritual reading. The allocation of the little free time available to priests proves, however, that practices of a spiritual nature were regularly considered even more important than study, further education, other sources of work, and recreation in all the years covered by the survey: 73% of priests organize their time in such a way that there is still room for spiritual activities; the percentage who find time within their hours of leisure for other activities deemed equally important is smaller. Finally, the survey findings show that, in terms of the proposed means for overcoming difficulties, the priest needs deep spiritual roots. In this case, prayer was most often cited as the most valuable help; it outranks conversations with brother priests, study, reading, and fourteen other possible ways of addressing problems (FBP Table A 49).

Obstacles to Spiritual Life

A spiritual life, however, is not something that falls ready-made into the priest's lap. From the replies to the question about activities over and above ministerial activities for which the priest has time (FBP Table A 48), it is clear that ideal and reality widely diverge with regard to spiritual activity. Prayer and meditation often disappear among many priests, because too much of their time is taken up with pastoral work: 34% had difficulty in finding the necessary time for it; 21% said there wasn't enough time for it; while 3% were so overburdened that, apart from their ministerial activities as priests, they had no time at all for anything else, and so there was no longer time for spiritual activity as such.

A further factor that may hinder the cultivation of spiritual life among priests clearly lies in their lack of spiritual preparation: only a few were able during their seminary years to aquire any adequate experience in this field (FBP Table A 71): only 53% could say yes to whether they had been taught ways of cultivating their spiritual life during their student years. That deserves notice, for it is in the very nature of spiritual life that its value can hardly be transmitted, still less deepened, through argumentation and deduction; it can only be revealed to the person who has actually "tasted" it (cf. 1 Pet 2:3). Here a very grave deficit persists in the formation of priests.

Too many commitments, too many administrative tasks, overburdening by pastoral tasks, and altogether a punishing schedule do not exactly favor, still less promote, the cultivation of spiritual life among priests. Indeed in too many cases they limit it or even rule it out entirely. If we start from the premise that a significant effect of prayer and meditation consists in bringing the world of faith into the routine of daily life, this restriction or suppression of spiritual exercises may seem less disastrous for priests than it is for laymen: for the priest's service repeatedly compels him—professionally, as it were—to engage with the world of faith, and here lies his spiritual advantage over the laity, who pursue a service in the secular world.

THE RELATIONSHIP TO GOD AS CRUX OF THE PROBLEM

One of the most powerful factors that "especially" determines and characterizes the priest in his service is "the wish to be there for others" (FBP Table A 52 and 53). The ideal of being available for others is then focused more particularly on people's anxieties. Priests overwhelmingly hold that, aside from generational problems (57%), these anxieties have to do with loss of faith (56%) and the gap between faith and daily life (in fourth place with 37%) (FBP Table A 50).

This assessment coincides with the replies given by priests concerning the reasons for the present crisis in the Church. The second largest percentage of replies identifies the cause in the decline of religious faith. So priests see the main reason for lapsed attendance at church in the "distance from God" of members of the Church.

It is only logical, therefore, that active secular priests should clearly assign first importance to evangelization: 79% express the view that the "sphere of activity of primary importance" lies here—compared with the 52% who cite liturgical and sacramental service and the 25% who speak of service to the community (FBP Table A 35). Supposing practical adherence to their own view of service, the majority of priests ought therefore strive to ensure through the preaching of the Gospel in their parishes that faith becomes increasingly rooted in daily life; consequently, priests would appear to be more concerned about the content of our faith that any other Christians. Fostering "access to God" and "friendship with Christ" through the opening or reinforcement of a personal relationship at the heart of faith is in their view the most important help they can offer to contemporary man. Priests evidently see the ultimate sense of their mission in their commitment to this goal; the compass needle of their service is pointed at it.

The Importance of the Question of God among Laity and Priests

If priests consider it imperative especially to provide "access to God" to the faithful in their pastoral ministry, they undoubtedly do so in response to one of the most demonstrable shortcomings within their communities. The question relating to this aspect is, however, posed in the wider context of questions about the priest's sense of alienation. Of the twenty-one possible problem areas proposed by the survey, the second most frequently checked box was the "question of God" (FBP Table A 37). In the survey report on "Church and Society" (see note 7), an interesting and very significant comparison is made in this problem area, from which we can draw some further conclusions here. The question was asked: "Once a contact is made and you are able to converse with someone who is well versed in questions of life and faith: what would you really like to speak with him about?" In replies by non-priests the question of God ranks only ninth among the fourteen themes proposed (FBS Table A 23). If we compare the replies of priests and laity, we find that priests have understood relatively well the value attached by the laity to other problems of faith (individual eschatology; natural science and faith; papal primacy; identity of the Catholic Church, etc.). Yet priests clearly overstate the importance of the question of God that burdens the laity. Have they perhaps projected their own difficulties onto those entrusted to their pastoral care? Do they declare the need for a personal relationship with God with such emphasis because the foundations of their own relationship with God are becoming increasingly insecure? Is the "crisis of God" especially widespread among priests?

Until now, the familiarity of the clergy with the truths of faith has generally been considered an advantage that priests enjoyed over the laity. But this advantage can be considerably relativized, given that professional preoccupation with the contents of the faith does not necessarily results in its integration into a priest's own life. These truths of the faith can also shrivel into trivialities of everyday life, without providing any élan to the priest's life. Yet another difficulty may further compound the difficulties priests have in incorporating truths of faith into real life: the fact that the preaching of the Word of God defines their role, and ensures them social and material security.

The survey on "Church and Society" in Germany discovered a phenomenon frequently commented on, that of "ritualists," admittedly a minority among Catholics, yet a "considerable" one (FBS 107ff.). The interpreter of the survey findings suggests that the phenomenon is confined to those whose connection with the Church is marked by a rather weak relationship with God, as measured by numerical data on participation in Mass. Undoubtedly it could easily be demonstrated that also in other cases of involvement in church-related social groupings, efforts to have a relationship with God and do his will clearly come second.

Other areas in the same survey confirm that the effort to understand life and service on the basis of a personal God was not equally strong among interviewees, and that this personal God as motivation for decision and attitude is outweighed by the force of experience. For example, only 36% of secular priests and 42% of religious priests identify "personal relationship to God" as the foundation on which they are especially "confirmed and supported in their service as priests." By contrast, 59% of the religious priests identify the "wish to be there for others" as the most important justification for their service. A similar attitude can be found among younger secular priests: 59% of them, too, identify the "wish to be there for others" as the main impulse for their service as priests; this is followed by "service to the parish" (54%), whereas the "personal relationship to God" only fifth among nine responses (FBP Tables A 52 and 53).

The ways in which priests overcome difficulties in their profession also enable us to recognize the dwindling ability of many priests to believe in a listening and ever-present God. Instead, priests turn increasingly to empirically ascertainable reality. Admittedly, "prayer" takes top place as the most valuable means for the overcoming of difficulties among all the secular and religious priests addressed by the questionnaire; yet for younger priests "conversation with friends" was seen as the more effective option (FBP Table A 49).

Factors that hamper personal relationship with God, together with the findings on applications for return to lay status cited above, show that the importance of the question of God for priests must be taken very seriously. For many priests it is now the central problem of their own faith. Tackling it means first raising awareness of the problem. It also means admitting the difficulties of finding dogmatic and objective data that bear upon the idea of God. Yet that in itself is not enough if we are to succeed in describing the traditional conception of spirituality, which as "subjective aspect of dogmatics" tries to understand faith as integral part and motivating force of life.

The "Imaginary" and the "Present" God

Eckehart Meister († 1327), the great German theologian and mystic, makes observations about the value of knowledge in reference to the question of God that can clarify and sharpen our perception of the problems we are trying to address here.[8] According to Eckehart Meister, our relationship to God can be directed at what he calls an "imaginary God" (*gedachter Gott*) (60). The term denotes a God reduced to a construct of the mind, a God distorted into an object of analysis and description. This God had in this way been turned into an actor whom man had dressed up in his own old and discarded clothes. So Eckehart Meister insists, man: "must get rid of your imaginary God . . ." (29 f.), "for when thought dies, so too does God" (60).

To name God in the third person clearly does not yet mean taking a step towards him: to think about God is also possible for those who have no hope in his salvation. Instead of that, Eckehart Meister stresses the need that each one seek "to have his God present." He "should accustom his mind to have God present at all times in feeling, in desire and in love" (59). The whole of his person should be penetrated by an "inner spiritual devotion" to the present God. "Whoever has God in his being in this way will take God divinely, and God shall shine forth on him in all things; for all things will taste of God to him, and God's image will be visible to him from all things . . . it's like someone who craves to drink: he may well want to do something else than drink, and he may well want to think of other things; but whatever he does, and with whomsoever he is, in whatever endeavor or whatever thoughts or whatever activity he is engaged, he cannot rid his mind of the idea of drink, so long as his thirst is not slaked; and the greater his thirst is, the more powerful and urgent and present and persistent is the idea of drink" (60f.).

---

[8] See *Eckehart Meister. Deutsche Predigten und Traktate*, edited and translated by Josef Quint, München, 1955; the page numbers interpolated in the text above refer to this edition. There are several English translations of Meister Eckhart: e.g., *Meister Eckhart: A Modern Translation*, transl. Raymond B. Blakney, New York: Harper and Row; *Meister Eckhart, The Essential Sermons, Commentaries, Treatises and Defense*, transl. and ed. by Bernard McGinn and Edmund Colledge, New York: Paulist Press, 1981; *Treatises and Sermons of Meister Eckhart*, New York: Octagon Books, 1983; *Meister Eckhart: Selected Writings*, ed. and transl. by Oliver Davies, London: Penguin Books, 1994.

To point the way to God is the noblest task of the priest's service. The understanding priests have of their service will show whether they wish primarily to increase knowledge of the contents of the faith, or whether on the contrary they strive to establish or deepen the act of faith itself, namely the personal conversion to the Father as the response to his act of salvation in Christ Jesus. Is the God they worship the God to whom they are totally devoted? Is he the "present God" to them? In other words, do they believe all their aspirations and actions to be aimed at revealing the true face of the Father of Jesus Christ, before whom every other reality in their lives is relativized?

The difference between the reality they encounter and the personal God must not of course be sharpened into alternatives; that would be neither theologically legitimate nor psychologically compelling. Nonetheless this difference remains real—and so the question is posed: Do priests live with, do they "reckon on," this personal God? Or do they lose more and more of this strength, so that they are in danger of thinking of God not as a person, but as an object—an "imaginary" God who slowly withers away below the scrutiny of what is empirical and tangible? Old and new insights on the priesthood pose this question anew; it ought not to be blurred by the presumption that this relationship to God in priests can be assumed to be implicitly present, or pre-supposed in a naïve way. Psychologists have long demonstrated "that our relationship to Him (God) can be forced."[9]

The findings I have cited from the survey on priests conducted in Germany leave no doubt in our mind that a constantly growing number of priests have ever more difficulty in experiencing God as present. They will all no doubt preserve him in the "imaginary" place reserved for him in the theological system handed down to them. But their ability "to grasp God in *all* things"[10] is slight. The consequence is that psychological, sociological, and political

---

[9] Viktor E. Frankl, *Der unbewußte Gott*. Wien, 2nd edn., 1949, 92.

[10] Meister Eckehart, cit. 59.

laws increasingly claim all the interest of priests and usurp God's place in their mind. The impetus to look beyond these laws, to look through them at the deeper truths of the faith, is gradually diminished or lost. The superficiality of the phenomenon is given priority; the hidden depths of faith are left in darkness. A larger number would admittedly still like to meet God wherever two or three are gathered in Christ's name (cf. Mt 18:20). But is that enough?

The existence of a community can be regarded as the *conditio sine qua non* for someone "to have God present." But if such a community were not to exist, and the witness of one's fellow Christians were not to compensate for the weakness of one's own faith, then this God would nowhere be found. Corresponding to this truth is the fact that in the survey mentioned it is especially the younger priests (FBP Table A 72) who lament their inability to seek the face of the Father in the depths of their own hearts and to cry "Abba! Father!" with the Spirit (Rom 8:15). Yet it is only by turning their gaze inwards, and trusting themselves to his guiding and protecting hand, that they can be sure of God's presence and thus find the divine impetus for the service to which they have been called.

SEEKING GOD'S FACE

"Service" itself is undoubtedly a valuable opportunity for the priest to develop a fruitful spiritual life. But service may also weaken instead of strengthen him. Though he is accustomed on a daily basis to have dealings with "the holy," he is no way relieved of the overriding need to "seek God's face" for the sake of his own faith. What means remain to him—other than his service? The means are those common to all the baptized, those that the Church offers to all her members for their sanctification; for the priest is incorporated in the community to which he belongs. The central challenge remains that arising from having been baptized. The communion that flows from baptism can—even if it is not directly experienced—support and stimulate him; and it demands of him a particular coherence: for with him rests the responsibility to awaken or deepen the readiness to be sanctified of the others who have been baptized by his own example and the authenticity of his own life and faith.

Prayer

Preaching, whose aim is to transmit God's Word, must be sustained by the preacher's encounter with God. Saint Augustine's *Confessions* or Anselm of Canterbury's *Proslogion* enable us to grasp this salvific connection: we can only do justice to talk *about* God on the basis of our ability to talk *to* him. Not without reason were listening to God's Word, dialogue with God in the Psalms, encounter with the wisdom of the Fathers of the Church, and prayer from the breviary promised by the candidate to the priesthood during his ordination. Life lived on the basis of faith, and the proclamation of this faith, are inseparably bound up with the presupposition of being *in* a relationship with God and not outside it. In this relationship alone the believer learns to recognize "that God shows himself willing to be his interlocutor, reveals himself as someone there: a familiar presence with whom he can converse."[11]

The survey findings show that the younger priests are, the more they lament the fact that, apart from their ministerial activity, they have "too little" or "practically no" time for "prayer, meditation, and reading," or "only with difficulty" find any time at all for it (FBP Table A 48). That such activity in individual cases should not only be necessary, but can also degenerate into routine, or be the consequence of inner unrest, or even a form of escapism, should not be ignored. Nevertheless the analysis developed here as a root cause is confirmed anew by this finding: A God, who remains "the nameless, the inscrutable hereafter of

---

[11] Jörg Splett, *Reden aus Glauben. Zum christlichen Sprechen von Gott.* Frankfurt, 1973, 24–47, here 29 and 42.

all things" is gradually disappearing. The mystery of God "must be called by name, invoked and loved, so that he remains there for us."[12]

A relationship with the present God, a relationship that is able to shape one's life, is threatened for many priests also in our own time. Pope Benedict leaves no doubt that priests have to seek communion with the Father in their fundamental devotion to Jesus Christ. Who helps them to practice this communion anew by invoking God, and to renew their own existence in a renewed certainty of his presence? They must learn this together, if they are to succeed in doing so alone.

Celebration of the Eucharist

Vatican II's Decree on the Ministry and Life of Priests (*Presbyterorum Ordinis*) especially stresses the Eucharist, "the source and summit of all preaching of the Gospel (*PO* 5)," as the main way of exposing them to the mystery of Christ. During their ordination the bishop had spoken to them: "Know what you do; imitate what you perform; since you celebrate the mystery of the death and resurrection of Christ, strive to overcome all evil and to transform it into new life." The Council fathers thus see the celebration of Mass as the central event in which priest's are configured to Christ the Priest and "daily offer themselves completely to God." "For this reason the daily celebration of it is earnestly recommended" (*PO* 13).

Clearly, however, in their formulation of the text, the Council fathers also recognized that the sacred celebration of the Eucharist in its daily repetition could be "abused." *Quotidiana vilescunt*—"daily events lose value," said the ancient Romans; familiarity breeds contempt, as we say in English. The context of the conciliar recommendation thus lays much stress on the need for personal dedication in the celebration: priests are reminded that "as ministers of the sacred mysteries, [they] act in a special

---

[12] Karl Rahner, *Von der Not und dem Segen des Gebetes*. Freiburg, 1958, 45f.

way in the person of Christ [. . .] And that is why they are invited to imitate what they handle." For "in the mystery of the eucharistic sacrifice, in which priests fulfill their principal function, the work of our redemption is continually carried out" (*PO* 13); and "by being nourished with Christ's Body they share in the charity of him who gives himself as food to the faithful" (*PO* 13). The decree repeatedly exhorts priests to be present in the celebration, heart and soul. So the Council fathers clearly recognized the underlying risk of falling into a mechanical routine. But they enunciate no theologically compelling reason for the daily celebration of the Eucharist.

The objection is valid; but still less, one might reply, is there any compelling reason *against* the priest's daily celebration of Mass. On the deepest level the Church in this way performs her own act of self-constitution: making Christ's self-oblation her own. This task demands an inner participation of particular commitment. Would "liturgy-free" days really be helpful to this? Why not through education and formation? Increasing the value of something by making it rare is more a sociological than a spiritual law. Saint Ignatius of Antioch, towering martyr of the early Church († *c*.135), wrote to the Ephesians, impressing on them the need for frequent communion: "Take heed, then, often to come together to give thanks to God, and show forth his praise. For when you assemble frequently in the same place, the powers of Satan are destroyed, and the destruction at which he aims is prevented by the unity of your faith."[13]

Benedict XVI, lastly, has repeatedly seized the opportunity to urge the daily celebration of Mass, especially when he addresses priests. "The ministerial priesthood was born at the Last Supper, together with the Eucharist, as my Venerable Predecessor John Paul II so frequently emphasized. 'All the more then must the life of the priest be "shaped" by the Eucharist' (Letter to Priests for Holy Thursday 2005, no. 1). In the first place, the devout, daily

---

[13] Saint Ignatius of Antioch, *Epistle to the Ephesians*, Chapter 13.

celebration of Holy Mass, the center of the life and mission of every priest, contributes to this goal."[14] The Pope urges this daily celebration—not out of duty, but for the sake of Christ.

Penance and Reconciliation

In discussing the holiness of priests, the question of the "Sacrament of Reconciliation" must finally be addressed.[15] Who is uninfluenced by the "crisis of the Sacrament of Penance"? Is not priests' appreciation of this sacrament prejudiced by the weak faith and scant practice of confession by the baptized?

The "forgetting" of this sacrament is nourished by various sources. Feuerbach, Marx, Comte, and Nietzsche all bequeathed to us categories of thought that promised to overcome the problem of evil with human means. The world, they taught, was to be rid of evil not by personal recognition of guilt, but by greater perspicacity, the reform of social conditions, and the influence of biological processes. Personal responsibility for human sin and error was dismissed or ignored. The "craze of innocence" (J.B. Metz) also spread in the Church.

Still other sources nourished this craze in parishes. For it is not always militant atheists who whitewash, or paper over, sin and guilt. A false interpretation of Revelation itself can be a prime cause: a neurotic empathy with the human condition can lead even priests to exonerate man from all the demanding claims of the Gospel, but in this way the Gospel of Jesus is robbed of all its salvific power. What man needs today is confirmation—not a state of uncertainty. The Christian commandment of our time seems to be: Accept yourself and accept others. For do not our contemporaries already have a heavy enough burden to bear without adding more to it? "Redemption means accepting yourself," proclaimed a Catholic priest in Rome a few years ago. And

---

[14] Address of Pope Benedict XVI at the end of the Eucharistic Concelebration with the Members of the College of Cardinals in the Sistine Chapel, April 20, 2005, no. 4.

[15] In my recent publication *Besiege das Böse mit dem Guten. Grenzen der Psychologie und die Kraft des Glaubens*, Augsburg, 2009, 81–107, I recently presented a kind of handbook for the individual confession of sins.

when later an itinerant missionary spoke in an Austrian parish of self-knowledge, guilt, and conversion, the parish priest curtly interrupted him: "For years I have been trying to convince the members of my community that they are good. And you speak about sin. You are completely ruining my pastoral efforts." Nieztsche went so far as to declare: "In the whole psychology of the 'evangel' the concept of guilt and punishment is lacking . . . , 'Sin,' any distance separating God and man, is abolished: precisely this is the 'glad tidings.'"[16]

"Does not modern man live under the threat of a darkening of conscience? A deformation of conscience? A clouding or deadening of conscience?" asked John Paul II on March 14, 1982. Not long afterwards, in October 1983, bishops from all over the world met for their Synod in Rome. For a whole month the bishops tried to refocus their gaze on the Sacrament of Reconciliation for the universal Church. The results of their deliberations were published by the Bishop of Rome on Advent Sunday 1984 in a remarkable and still noteworthy document, the Post-Synodal Apostolic Exhortation *Reconciliatio et Paenitentia*, Reconciliation and Penance in the Mission of the Church Today. The Saint of the Confessional, Jean Marie Vianney, is also referred to in it. And the particular concern of the Holy Father was "to recall the principal aspects of this Great Sacrament" (no. 28).

As I have suggested above, the number of those eager to be converted, who set out on the road to the Curé d'Ars, is something of a miracle in itself.[17] Under normal circumstances, hardly anyone goes willingly to confession. The theologian and popular writer J. Wittig († 1949) asked himself as a child: "Why didn't Jesus Christ also redeem us from confession, seeing he had already redeemed us?"[18] So the crisis of the Sacrament of Penance, which the synod had acknowledged, will not be removed

---

[16] Friedrich Nietzsche, *The Antichrist*, 33, quoted from *The Portable Nietzsche*, edited and translated by Walter Kaufmann. New York: The Viking Press, 1954, 606.

[17] See my introductory remarks on the Curé d'Ars above, vii–xiii.

[18] Joseph Wittig, *Die Erlösten*. Hochland 19 (1921/22), 1–26.

by itself. John Paul II's Apostolic Exhortation urges catechesis and preaching, and still more "a pastoral ministry of penance and reconciliation." Already Vatican II had taught that priests "are united with the intention and the charity of Christ when they administer the sacraments. They do this in a special way when they show themselves to be always available to administer the Sacrament of Penance whenever it is reasonably requested by the faithful" (PO 13). The opportunity to receive the sacrament ought to be made as easy as possible, to prevent the practice being limited unnecessarily by issues of scheduling and the like. And above all: the priest himself must receive the sacrament. He can only preach in a credible way what he himself practices in his life; he will only create opportunities for others if he himself seeks the opportunity to confess.

THE PRIEST—
NO INDIVIDUAL FIGHTER

In this context of a spirituality nourished by the practise of the evangelical counsels, I would like to invite all priests, during this year dedicated to them, to welcome the new springtime which the Spirit is now bringing about in the Church, not least through the ecclesial movements and the new communities. "In his gifts the Spirit is multifaceted . . . He breathes where he wills. He does so unexpectedly, in unexpected places, and in ways previously unheard of . . . but he also shows us that he works with a view to the one body and in the unity of the one body." In this regard, the statement of the Decree (*Presbyterorum Ordinis*) continues to be timely: "While testing the spirits to discover if they be of God, priests must discover with faith, recognize with joy and foster diligently the many and varied charismatic gifts of the laity, whether these be of a humble or more exalted kind." These gifts, which awaken in many people the desire for a deeper spiritual life, can benefit not only the lay faithful but the clergy as well. The communion between ordained and charismatic ministries can provide "a helpful impulse to a renewed commitment by the Church in proclaiming and bearing witness to the Gospel of hope and charity in every corner of the world."

—Pope Benedict XVI, Letter Proclaiming a Year
for Priests 2009–2010, June 16, 2009

The following reflections do not discuss specific models of spiritual life, as might be implied by the title of this chapter. I am not concerned here with an opposition, or clash, between different kinds of spirituality—for instance, between a communal spirituality corresponding to the Rule of Saint Benedict and a spirituality oriented to the individual, like that promoted by the Exercises of Saint Ignatius. Nor do I propose to compare the community-based devotion of those in the religious life with that of secular priests, which in general concerns the individual. Rather, I wish here to tackle the question: Does the conception of spirituality, as it is encountered among priests today, take sufficient note of the potential values of community awareness? Has their spirituality aroused a sense of community, i.e., the sense of togetherness that consecrated persons share? Or, to put the question the other way round: What does the community factor contribute to spiritual fulfillment? Is the sense of community helpful for the priest's spirituality? Does it perhaps have a boundary, a limit, here and there?

THE CONTEMPORARY NEED
FOR COMMUNITY

No kind of spirituality, whatever particular emphases it has, is drawn up, as it were, on the theological 'drawing board' from a single basic concept. Each form of spirituality absorbs new elements into its life and undergoes change. The boundaries between their different forms of expression are also fluid. Spirituality therefore is open to values important to a particular period, which in many cases is rediscovering them. That goes also for our own time.

Undoubtedly today it is not so much the individualizing of the personality, but human communion that is sought and presented as an ideal. Clearly the sense of community and solidarity are commonly recognized as a virtue; the yearning for community is a need strongly and widely felt. Horst-Eberhard Richter, Director of the Center for Psychosomatic Medicine at the University of

Giessen, recognized this need in his work. Years ago he explained in an interview that solidarity had been developed as a logical principle in opposition to the urge of rivalry and individualism. Ever more people, he recognized, were convinced that growing competition in the struggle for greatness, power, and possession would end in the destruction of all. In addition, people were fearful of being more and more oppressed by the power of institutions and bureaucracies. Such ideas "suggested a change in the way people feel about life. People are gradually losing hope of being able to find a reality as an individual made in the image and likeness of God and more and more moving to the idea that man can only develop himself as an individual in association with others and that man only has a chance to develop his potential by living in communion with others."[1]

A superficial consideration of some sociological and psychological laws that are operative in regulating relationships between the individual and the community would be enough to confirm such analyses and throw further light on the reasons for this need for community. At the same time, responses to this need can be identified, for instance, in the hopes placed in the group and what it ought, and under favorable circumstances is no doubt able, to perform.

From his origins man has lived neither as a self-referential individual being—no man is an island—nor in the anonymous mass: man sees himself as a social animal, primarily as member of a family, and secondarily of a circle of friends. He is thus incorporated in a structured social organization, between isolation on the one hand and amorphous disorganization on the other. Man suffers from a very significant loss of human fulfillment if he lacks the support of this structure.

So the group can help the individual to overcome a sense of anomie, of loss of sense of direction, and win him for social objectives and guiding values. By incorporation in the community

---

[1] Horst-Eberhard Richter, *Evangelische Kommentare*, November 1974, 683–686, here 683.

man's vulnerability can be healed, his inner conflicts "removed." The expectations that others have of him already make for positive reactions. As far as his conduct is concerned, readiness and expectations are then reinforced. If the group transmits to its members the need "*to be true to themselves*," they are *true to themselves*.[2]

And the further question is posed: How can man develop and maintain feelings of self-esteem without reference to the community? Man's judgment of his own abilities and his own ideas remains unstable and mutable without social endorsement. The group thus becomes an important *conditio since qua non* for the individual's consciousness of his own value and justifiably seems to many people a value in itself. Relationship with the community seems, in particular, indispensable for the finding and strengthening of self-identity. How, other than in the community, can man succeed in winning respect for his achievements, and, on that basis, in being recognized "as a person whose gradual growth and self-transformation have meaning in the eyes of those who are beginning to have meaning for him"?[3]

If human self-assurance is thus achieved with the help of the group, it follows that self-identity is not developed in solitude; it does not, it cannot, grow from the isolated individual, but requires a relationship with society. It is developed in the relationship between something that is innate in the individual and an essential aspect of the inner coherence of a group in which the individual has his place. The term *identity* thus expresses a reciprocal relationship, since it comprises both a lasting inner correspondence with self and a lasting participation in particular traits specific to the community, of which the human individual is a member. This reciprocity is the condition for the individual's fulfillment in life. It is an ongoing, not a temporary, relationship and this in itself implies that the formation of identity is not completed at a particular age. It is rather a lifelong development, which often

---

[2] Dieter Claessens, *Instinkt—Psyche—Geltung*. Köln, 2nd edn, 1970, 171.
[3] The following discussion rests on Eric Homburger Erikson, *Identität und Lebenszyklus*, Frankfurt, 1966, 123–212.

proceeds without the individual and his society being aware of it. That is why the formation of one's identity cannot be taken for granted even in adulthood and old age. In this period of life, too, it consists in the close correspondence of central aspects of the individual self with those of the community. Isolation, self-absorption, and disgust with life can only be kept in check if the action of the individual meets with an answering echo in the social context.

In our opening remarks we suggested that spirituality is not developed in a vacuum: it also reflects the Zeitgeist. It is placed in the context of currents and movements of the time. It ought not to be, indeed cannot be, blind to anthropological insights. In whatever specific mold it is conceived, it ought not to ignore or underestimate the widespread and growing awareness of the value and the amply confirmed power of society in our time. Pope Benedict XVI exhorts priests to seek unity of purpose and foster mutual help.

Communion Confirmed by the Revelation

Those who take seriously the widespread human yearning for community ought not to be accused of leaping aboard a bandwagon or conforming to a fad. It is both theologically correct and pastorally necessary to create space for "communion" in the realm of faith and in Christian life. Faith, if it is to be translated into experience, if it is to be realized, demands community and is wholly aimed at its expression in a community. It even presupposes the creation of communion among men as the measure of its authenticity. For the Church describes herself "as sign and instrument of communion with God and of unity among all men" (*LG* 1). Back in 1937 Henri de Lubac repudiated the accusation that the practice of faith led to isolation: "We are accused of being individualists, by virtue of our faith, and even against our will—whereas in reality Catholicism in its innermost being is inherently social (i.e., aimed at society)."[4]

---

[4] Henri de Lubac, *Katholizismus als Gemeinschaft*. Einsiedeln, 1943, 15.

God's salvific action is directed not to man in isolation but man in association and hence in some sense to the group. Rarely does the individual evangelist, acting alone, proclaim what God has done. The bearers of the Word come from a community and desire to win others for a community. Faith thus builds up the community and needs the community for its fulfillment. Exegesis thus identified the people of the Old Covenant as having the character of God's People and described the indissoluble unity between the individual and the community with the term "corporate personality."[5] The initial chapters of the First Letter of Peter make it clear that the response to God's act of election in the New Covenant can only happen at the community level: the redeemed live their priesthood in their *common* witness of the faith among non-believers. How, after all, can the theological affirmation of the "Body of Christ" be realized other than as a community? The apostle Paul wishes in this image to distinguish and interpret the indissoluble intellectual and spiritual solidarity of the local Church. But if we are to understand this image in the right way, we must realize that community of faith is not conceived by Saint Paul as an abstract quantity. It is no semantic or terminological hypostasis. On the contrary, it is a dimension of faith that the faithful must experience in a particular place, in other words, with reference to particular men and women and a particular social environment. It follows that the specific Christian community, rooted in a particular place and time, can never be replaced by otherwordly inwardness or by a purely notional outreach to the largely intangible universal Church.

This dependence of the individual believer on society is shown not only by the major lines of the history of salvation. Individual references in the New Testament also testify to this basic law of our faith. The apostle to the Gentiles thus gives a striking testimony of his personal social sense in his Letter to the Romans: "For I long to see you, that I may impart to you some

---

[5] Cf. Josef de Fraine, *Adam und seine Nachkommen.* Köln, 1962, 178 and 225 ff.

spiritual gift to strengthen you, that is, that we may be mutually encouraged by each other's faith, both yours and mine" (Rom 1:11–12). Paul here seems to give an ideal description of the emotional bond that attaches the individual to the community; there is reciprocity in the relationship between them: each needs the other. The apostle testifies to the gifts of the Spirit to fill the community with courage and consolation. The community gains in strength, when Paul takes it up.

But Paul does not come as a giver alone. He becomes conscious that he has already emphasized himself too much with his announcement of communicating the gift of the Spirit. He therefore very speedily relativizes his precedence as apostle vis-à-vis the community and recognizes that for him too social communion with the community is a gift. The encouragement that his stay in the community will bring with it is to the benefit of giver and receiver. It is produced by the faith in which all members of the community meet each other, which they express together and which they mutually confess to each other. Only in the community can there be mutual encouragement; only in the community can its members give one another fresh heart.

Saint Paul is not shy about expressing his longing to meet the community. The law of the history of salvation does not impede the emotional and human level or exclude it. Quite the contrary: it is through this emotionally charged encounter that the gift of the Spirit is accepted and the salvific act consummated. This is shown by other passages in Paul's letters, which similarly express the apostle's longing to meet with other Christian communities, and express the strong human bond that attaches him to his fellowmen, and in which Paul employs similarly emotional, heartfelt language. "But now that Timothy has come to us from you, and has brought us the good news of your faith and love and reported that you always remember us kindly and long to see us, as we long to see you . . . praying earnestly night and day that we may see you face to face and supply what is lacking in your faith" (1 Thess 3: 6, 10; cf. also 2 Tim 1:3f.).

Dietrich Bonhoeffer, summing up his thoughts about the nature of Christian community based on the common life that he and his seminarians had experienced together in the preacher's seminary at Finkenwalde, refers to both these latter Pauline letters and concludes: "So the Christian needs his fellow-Christian, who tells him God's Word. He needs him again and again, whenever he is uncertain and disheartened; for he cannot help himself alone, without betraying the truth. He needs his brother as bearer and proclaimer of God's Word of salvation. His needs his brother for the sake of Jesus Christ alone. The Christ in his own heart is weaker than the Christ in the words of his brother; the one is uncertain, the other is certain. The goal of all communion between Christians thus becomes at the same time clear: they meet each other as bringers of the Gospel of salvation."[6]

Communion of the Baptized in the Footsteps of Mary

Men and women who have received the gift of the Spirit have repeatedly emphasized the relationship of the Christian with his fellow-Christians as a source of mutual encouragement. This relationship holds good for all the faithful. In past times a raised sanctuary may have isolated the priest, but today he is more likely to stand with his back to the wall and be blamed for the failures of others near and far. And such "exposure" may lead to his isolation and loneliness. We have had painful reminders that an idealized concept of the self-sufficient and unassailable personality was hardly applicable to every priest in the past; yet it is especially now that most of them feel a need for social involvement.

The theological breakthrough in this sense came with Vatican II. The Constitution on the Church *Lumen Gentium* and the Decree on the Ministry and Life of Priests (*Presbyterorum Ordinis*) both express the truth that the priest is in the first place

---

[6] Dietrich Bonhoeffer, in: *Bonhoeffer-Auswahl*, Vol. 3. München, 1970, 148. Bonhoeffer summed up his experiences of Christian community in the preacher's seminary at Finkenwalde in his book *Gemeinsames Leben*, first published in German in 1939 and first translated into English as *Life Together* in 1954; a paperback edition was published by HarperOne in 1978.

a believer among believers, part of the People of God like each of the baptized: "priests ... live with the rest of men as with brothers" (*PO* 3). The fact that priests, in their responses to questionnaires, stress the importance of their relationship with fellow-Christians in particular and with their fellowmen in general corresponds to this theological truth.

After several decades of placing particular emphasis upon knowledge and the doctrine of the faith as key elements for the transmission of the faith and pastoral ministry, the Church's pastors and educators rediscovered the power of feeling: the status of the "*communio affectiva*—the non-intellectual social bond"— once again came to the fore. Even if this human capacity must always be subordinated to the control of reason,[7] its importance for human decisions is enormous. Saint Augustine († 430) maintained: "Our feet on this way are, namely, our affections. According to the affections that everyone has, according to the love that everyone experiences, man draws closer to or distances himself from God."[8] Such supports for faith are especially perceptible and effective in the circle of the like-minded. In his letter proclaiming a Year for Priests, inaugurated on the Solemnity of the Most Sacred Heart of Jesus, June 19, 2009, Pope Benedict XVI did not neglect to recall the "new springtime which the Spirit is now bringing about in the Church, not least through the ecclesial movements and the new communities" as sources from which priests could strengthen their faith.

That is the case—to cite just one or two examples—when the priests of the Focolare founded by Chiara Lubich exchange experiences and discuss spiritual and human questions with other members of their movement. The various branches of the Apostolic Movement of Schönstatt founded by Father Joseph Kentenich draw inspiration from mutual prayer, contemplation, and planning in their common devotion to the Blessed Virgin Mary.

---

[7] Cf. the present author's '*Communio*. Utopie oder Programm?,' in *Quaestiones disputatae* 148, Freiburg, 1993, 43ff.

[8] Augustine of Hippo, En. Ps. 94,2 (CChr. SL 39, 1331, 31ff.).

The priests of the Neocatechumenal Way also take part in "community days" that bring together all the members of their groups; they cooperate with the laity in preparing the daily celebration of the Word of God or the Sunday liturgy; they rediscover together with the laity that their shared sanctification from baptism is the source of fruitful service for their priesthood. Or we may recall those priests who seek to pursue the way of Charismatic Renewal with groups or in personal parishes: they "refuel" their spiritual life in open prayer meetings and strengthen their own faith and hope in prolonged sessions of praise. For many ordained persons their postconciliar integration in Catholic lay groups of this kind has proved a great blessing. They are a privileged opportunity to experience more readily the classic definition of friendship "*idem sentire, idem velle*—to feel the same, to will the same."

In comparison with other religions and sometimes even with other Christian confessions, we suddenly encounter here a wonderful peculiarity of our Catholic faith: the fact that it so willingly embraces our natural hopes, experiences, and yearnings. It does not ridicule them, is not suspicious of them, does not dismiss them out of hand. It builds with our feelings the practice of our faith: ceremonial vestments and incense turn the liturgy into a sublime theatrical performance; music and songs lift our heart and inspire feelings of jubilation; pilgrimages on foot discipline our body and give us a taste for sacrifice and atonement.

So it is no wonder that the Church accepts and applauds man's yearning for the Mother. She invites us to accept the Mother of God as our Mother.

Yet it is not as if the Church had deduced this from pedagogical principles! The Lord himself willed that it should be so. He wished that our natural emotions, the promptings of our heart, should encourage our way to God. Indeed, in his dying moments on the Cross he expressly entrusted his Mother to us: "Woman, behold your son," he said to Mary, referring to John. "Behold, your Mother" (Jn 19:26), he then said to his disciple, referring to her, the Virgin of Nazareth. And the words he spoke to John from the Cross are addressed to us all. There is no doubt that the Lord with this injunction to "behold your Mother" wished to establish a quite intimate bond between his Mother and each one of us.

Was this just a sop to our childishness, a sentimental bonbon so to say? In itself the agony on the Cross, the moment of Christ's death, stands in utter contradiction to any such idea: the misunderstanding that the Mother of God is a concession to our puerile religious feeling; that the establishment of a relationship with her is a way of exploiting our innate sentimentality; or even a way of pandering to the egoism that lies in our practice of faith: that the Virgin Mary is a convenient way of purging us of the difficulties and resistance, just as we were accustomed to having our natural mother do; that she may make our life as trouble-free and pleasant as possible. Quite the opposite: Jesus' starting point is our natural sense of the maternal arising from the relationship with our own mother. If we experience this relationship in a selfish way, it must be purified. The core of this relationship is not sentimental but of demanding severity: Mary leads our devotion to her beyond herself.

Communion among Secular Priests

Undoubtedly communion with his fellow Christians becomes for the priest a reliable support for his service and for his own sanctification. The experience of the Christian community, and of the exchange of faith with members of the parish and of lay associations, has indeed become so precious for many presbyters that they cannot imagine their life without it. Despite that, there are good grounds to question the conclusion that meetings and dialogue with his fellow-Christians are merely a way of satisfying the priest's need for community. For frequently all these social occasions become opportunities for service; the priest feels they are part of his pastoral responsibility.

As mentioned above, however, community is sought by modern man precisely to relieve him from the tensions of his professional life and from repressions of all kinds. The same goes for the priest: the collection of activities for which the presbyter remains mainly responsible gives rise in him to a thirst for community. He seeks opportunities to communicate freely: social encounters without rivalry, and freedom, or relaxation, from the hectic activities of his professional life; social occasions in which service is not on the agenda and he is accepted as a fellow human being and fellow Christian. That the community does not coincide with the working group of priests is advantageous for the priest: the exchange of faith ought not to be confused with working arrangements, nor spirituality with pastoral planning.

The common sharing of basic existential experiences makes communion appear meaningful, indeed, sometimes downright necessary, to priests. The not insignificant problem of their theological and human identity cannot be considered any more resolved today than it was in the past. Indeed it has been posed anew by a development in the Church that has given the image of the priest wholly new contours. No one ought to discredit the theological progress made by Vatican II in clarifying the question of the ordained ministry or dispute the need to trace back the theology of ministry in the Church to its roots in Holy Scripture. But in considering the new identity of the presbyter in the postconciliar Church we cannot avoid being confronted by the question of the so-called democratization of the Church, as exemplified by the rampantly developed system of councils at the various levels of the Church, the rapid expansion of the *Katholikentage* (Catholic congresses) in Germany and similar events at the ecumenical level, or the progressive delegation of pastoral services to the laity. What has all this brought to priests in terms of reinforcing a sense of their own identity and the consciousness of their own mission? Assemblies of vicariates foranes rarely take place now without the participation of the laity, for whom such questions as priest's dress, the obligation to pray from the breviary, celibacy, or the administration of the Sacrament of Penance are not supremely important. In the search for new structures, the Church has encouraged wider lay and professional participation: and in such structures priests find themselves face to face with professionals—professionals not of evangelization but of management consultancy. All these new developments may have sprung from an indispensable *aggiornamento*. Yet for many the process begun in this way has diminished the image of the priest, and priests have difficulty to adjusting to the watered-down identity that results.

The new image of the priest certainly does not succeed if it falls into the hands of iconoclasts, still less when it is presented by self-styled public sages. Eric Homburger Erikson has pointed out that, for example, the question of what psychoanalysis is or is not is rooted in the value that it retains for the psychoanalyst himself, since a precise psychoanalytical identity has become the cornerstone of his existence as man and scientist.[9] Now, as in the past, priests frequently view such basic psychological laws with contempt. Undoubtedly difficulties, the organization of work and pastoral planning, pose problems for a priest; but, for him, even more important than overcoming them should be the elaboration of a professional and human identity. And this has become all the harder for him today, because that identity is no longer supported at the social or cultural level.

That is why periods of shared isolation or retreat would be desirable for priests. In such interludes it is possible to create "microclimatic conditions" that are not admitted in the socio-climatic environment of our time. A distancing from environmental pressures could thus be achieved, along with self-affirmation fostered not just by social environment and instinct alone but by the group reflection of others who are themselves directly concerned.[10] The clarification of the image of the priest achieved in such group reflection, appropriating theological findings, does not ignore the need to form and deepen self-identity.

---

[9] Erik Homburger Erikson, op. cit. (note 3) 195 f.
[10] Cf. Dieter Claessens, op. cit. (note 2) 171f.

Responsible churchmen of the past may have placed too much emphasis on the ideal of the parish priest as the individual champion of the Gospel, the single evangelizer, the secret agent acting alone. But the model of the "007 of the Gospel" finds a remarkable contradiction in the evidence of the New Testament. Pastoral theology in its classical sense already recognized the *regula socii*.

In his study on "paired mission in the New Testament"[11] Joachim Jeremias pointed out that most New Testament witnesses worked in pairs: indeed Jesus specifically sent them forth in pairs. The twelve disciples (Mark 6:7) were sent out "two by two" to preach the Gospel; likewise the seventy-two other disciples (Lk 10:1) appointed by the Lord "were sent ahead of him, two by two." The pairing of the disciples is also found in the lists of the names of the twelve disciples in Matthew (10:2–4) and Luke (6:12–16; cf. also Acts 1:13). This is all the more striking since the grouping of the twelve in six pairs of witnesses could obscure the eschatological significance of this circle of disciples and its participation in the Last Judgment at the end of time, when the significance of the number twelve is further emphasized: when the Son of Man shall sit in judgment "you who have followed me will also sit on twelve thrones, judging the twelve tribes of Israel" (Mt 19:28). Why were the disciples named in pairs? The reason doubtless lies in the fact that, according to Jewish law, a testimony is validated only if confirmed by two witnesses.

It is striking that a similar pairing of apostles is also found in the apostolic Church. So we find the apostles in the first Christian community in Jerusalem preaching, or sent on mission, not individually but in pairs, for example Peter and John (Acts 3:1, 8:14); Paul and Barnabas (15:22); Judas and Silas (15:27). The Christian community in Antioch also seems to have acted in this way: there we find the apostle pairs Paul and Barnabas (Acts 11:30; Gal 2:1); Barnabas and Mark (Acts 15:39); Paul

---

[11] Joachim Jeremias, *Abba. Studien zur neutestamentlichen Theologie und Zeitgeschichte.* Göttingen, 1966, 132–139.

and Silas (Acts 15:40). Furthermore, several introductions to the Pauline letters contain references to "partners," "fellow workers," "fellow servants in the Lord" (cf. Rom 16:21; 2 Cor 8:23): in the first and second letter to the Thessalonians the fellow-worker is Silas; in the second letter to the Corinthians, in the letters to the Philippians and to the Colossians, it is Timothy. This practice, no doubt customary among Jews, seems to have become general throughout the early Church. Yet evidence for it can also be found in Gentile-Christian communities. So the Pauline communities clearly seem to have acted in the same way (cf. 2 Cor 8:16ff.).[12] Moreover, Paul himself seems repeatedly to have adopted the custom of sending out apostles in pairs for his apostolate: Timothy and Erastus (Acts 19:22); Titus and his brother (2 Cor 12:18); Tychicus and Onesimus (Col 4:7–9); Zenas and Apollos (Tit 3:13).

According to the biblical evidence, however, there seems to have been another reason for the sending out of apostles in pairs, other than the legal form customary among Jews. It seems to lie in the content of the Gospel itself. For the apostle, the messenger, had the task of preaching the Gospel of Christ crucified, which was "a stumbling block to Jews and folly to Gentiles" (1 Cor 1:23). He was given the task of preaching the Gospel of Jesus' victory over death that fell on dead ears, and not only in the Areopagus in Athens (Acts 17:16ff.). Quite clearly he needed a witness, not only to strengthen the faith of others but also to strengthen his own faith; for Paul too the Gospel is not something hermetically sealed; it was a treasure borne "in earthen vessels" (2 Cor 4: 7).

The priest, who is given the task of bearing witness to the Good News in this world, needs the faith of his consecrated brothers and sisters. It is only by acting together that the faithful can continually lay hold in prayer and dialogue upon the guidance of the Gospel for their service and their life. Pope Benedict asks

---

[12] Joachim Jeremias considers it self-evident "with almost all commentators" that the names mentioned in Acts 20:4 represent apostle pairs; cf. op. cit. 138.

us priests to be "a model and inspiration for the community" through "brotherly unity and love."

SAFEGUARDING INDIVIDUAL FREEDOM

Feeling and consciousness direct man in our time to the need for communion. But communion can only succeed if it does not overstep, or usurp, the intrinsic value and dignity of the individual. That is why none of the members of a group should ever be "collectivized," i.e., forcefully conscripted into a collective organization. Here I cannot go into the whole problem that arises from any overaccentuation of group thought and that makes many experiments powered by group dynamics suspect. Social psychologists justly describe such attempts as "social overdetermination of the individual" (Philipp Lersch).

The yearning for communion and the contribution it makes to the growth of faith should not therefore be absolutized—neither for the baptized nor for the ordained. Only in the tension between the social dimension and individuality does man reach maturity, including maturity in faith; neither the one nor the other pole should dominate him. A fruitful reciprocity needs to be found between man as an individual, whose individual freedom is sacrosanct, and man as a social animal, who can only mature by entering into society. And it is in this reciprocity that community as a help for the priest's way of faith also finds its limit.

III

⚜

LIMITATIONS

8

NO REDUCTION
OF THE MINISTRY OF PRIESTS
TO LITURGY

What has become the classical conception of the priesthood in Catholicism, its centering in the Eucharist (*sacerdos—sacrificium*), is one opposed to the primacy of the Word that hitherto had been considered typically Protestant. Of course, a concept of the priesthood based on the primacy of the Word cannot in any way be considered necessarily anti-sacramental. Vatican II's Decree on the Ministry and Life of Priests (*Presbyterorum Ordinis*) proves quite the contrary. At this point the question is posed: How far do the alternatives just described exclude each other and how far can they mutually cross-pollinate each other and so be mutually enriching? The basic question that Vatican II faced was this: How far can the classical Tridentine image of the priest be broadened and developed by taking into account the demands of the Reformation, of critical exegesis, and of the different context of modern life, without losing the essential? Vice versa, how far can the Protestant idea of "ministry" absorb the living tradition of the Catholic Church, both of the East and of the West? For as far as the priesthood is concerned, there is, after the Council of Trent, no essential difference between Catholicism and Orthodoxy.

—*Cardinal Joseph Ratzinger, Ministry and Life of Priests,*
Lecture to the Congregation for the Clergy, October 24, 1995

CORRECTION OF THE TRIDENTINE IMAGE OF THE PRIEST

During the Synod of Bishops in the Federal Republic of Germany (1972–75) there was some discussion of whether it was appropriate to authorize the laity also to preach during the celebration of the Eucharist. So a resolution was drafted on this matter. Bearing the title "The participation of the laity in preaching," it granted authority to preach during the celebration of the Eucharist, and, when put to the vote, was accepted by a majority of the synodal Fathers. Soon afterwards the Code of Canon Law of 1983 prescribed in Canon 767: "The most important form of preaching is the homily, which is part of the liturgy itself, and is reserved to a priest or deacon."

What, we may ask, are the theological grounds for this canonical prescription? This is a question that also affects pastoral practice found in the German-speaking area, which here and there continues to have difficulty in observing and implementing the canonical regulation adopted for the Church as a whole. "Authority to preach without ordination" not only contradicts the Code of Canon Law now in force in the Church, but is also substantially at variance with the theology of ministry in the Church.

SACRAMENTALLY SENT—ALSO TO PREACH

An examination of the process of drafting that led to the conciliar Decree on the Ministry and Life of Priests (*Presbyterorum Ordinis*) shows that the presbyter's task of preaching is more than a canonical mission (*missio canonica*) authorized by the law of ordination of the universal Church. For it arises from the innermost nature of consecration itself. This is especially shown by the process of formulation of the Decree that finally led in its final version to the account of the function of priests as ministers of God's Word (*PO* 4): The authorization given to priests to preach God's Word is rooted in the presbyter's fundamental relationship to Christ and to his Gospel founded in the act of ordination itself; it is not derived from some authority to preach specific to the bishop nor is it simply a juridical concession conferred by the "social body of the Church."

Not least, the drawing up of the Decree during the Council and its results are of great significance in the history of theology, because in them the one-sided, since anti-Lutheran, formulations of the Council of Trent received a significant supplement.

First, in relation to the theological thinking of the Council Fathers, one must note the fundamental fact that it was no longer acceptable to oppose to each other two factors of equal weight in regard to empowerment for spiritual agency, namely, the authority given by ordination and the authority given by canon law. According to this new position adopted by the Council, the sending forth of the minister essentially flows from ordination itself. The juridical act associated with it is to be interpreted simply as assignment to the pastoral field. It follows therefore that the bishop cannot simply delegate *ex auctoritate sua* the task of preaching during the celebration of the Eucharist. Such delegation must rather depend on whether the recipient of the delegation is qualified to preach by means of ordination. If not, the bishop would have to ignore the grace conferred by ordination and replace it by an enactment based on canon law. Any delegation by the bishop must on the contrary be based on the premise of ordination, which has been made possible by God and is supported by the prayer of the community.

IS EVERYONE RESPONSIBLE FOR PREACHING?

The advocates of extending to the laity authority to preach during the celebration of the Eucharist base their case on the responsibility of the whole Christian community for the transmission of the Word of God. The apostle Paul is said to support their case with his statement: "For as often as you eat this bread and drink the cup, you proclaim the Lord's death until he comes" (1 Cor 11:26). Leading exegetes contradict this interpretation: they base their case either on the recognition that the eucharistic event as such is "proclamation of the Lord" (Heinrich Schlier), or on the claim that Paul had in mind a verbal proclamation with the help of the Word (Hans Conzelmann). In neither the one nor the other, however, does authorization for each individual member of the faithful to take over preaching during Mass arise from this verse; for the task or faculty given to the whole community cannot—according to an axiom of logic—be fulfilled by an individual member of it.[1] Nor can it be ignored, finally, that Paul, in his preaching of the Gospel, claimed a high authority for himself in his dealing with the various Christian communities. This authority assumed by the apostle decisively modified the responsibility of the communities (e.g., in his relationships with the Galatians or with the Corinthians); and the Pastoral Letters leave no doubt that it is the responsibility of the *ministry* to guard what has been entrusted to it, namely, the preaching of the Gospel and its dissemination (cf. 1 Tim 6:20; 2 Tim. 1:12 f.).

So the office of preaching in the Church is not entrusted to all "preachers" in the same way. Responsibility for different forms of spreading the Gospel is incumbent on individual participants in mission: proclaiming the Good News to the community and the acceptance of this proclamation by the community are not one and the same. We thus read in Vatican II's Constitution on the Sacred Liturgy *Sacrosanctum Concilium*: "Although the sacred liturgy is principally the worship of the divine majesty it likewise contains much instruction for the faithful. For in the liturgy God speaks to his people, and Christ is still proclaiming his Gospel. And the people reply to God both by song and by prayer" (no. 33).

---

[1] *A collectivo ad distributivum non valet illatio*—An individual obligation cannot be deduced from a collective one.

What Does "Preaching" Mean?

Not least, the transmission of the Word of God in the Church needs to be defined precisely. If what is meant is simply "service to the Word," we ought not immediately to speak of "preaching"; otherwise a separation would take place that would lead to a one-dimensional concept of preaching. The Lord is himself the subject of preaching, and not just the historical origin or the object of *kerygma*. Rather he proclaims himself when the preacher speaks in his person: "He who hears you hears me" (Lk 10:16). It is Christ himself who speaks through the medium of the Holy Spirit infused in the preacher. So preaching is a charismatic act. In the act of preaching the Lord (*kyrios*) works through his Sprit (*pneuma*) by the speech of his messenger. So the latter does not presume to speak of anything that has not been wrought through him by Christ (cf. Rom 15:18).

Alongside its source in Christ, it is thanks to the Church that preaching takes place. Preachers are not self-appointed: they are sent. The apostle Paul writes to the community in Rome: "And how are they to believe in him of whom they have never heard? And how are they to hear without a preacher?" (10:15). Only he whom the Church legitimates as someone belonging to her is authorized to preach. In this sense, not only does the *kerygma* precede the Church, but the Church precedes the *kerygma*. It is in the Church that the "presence of Christ in the Word" (H. Schlier) is perpetuated.

This happens preeminently in the central locus of preaching: the liturgy. For here God's presence becomes real with incomparable density. When in the eucharistic celebration "the perceptible sign of the sermon" can be heard alongside the "visible Word of the Sacrament," then God himself is at work in his Son. In preaching, the preacher does not draw from his own resources, neither as the mouthpiece of the Word nor as the transmitter of the sign: he acts in the person of Christ himself. Only respect for this relationship can support the faith in such a way that salvation is truly worked in the word and in the sign, even in the case of apparently contradictory earthly experiences.

According to the faith of the Church, the relationship of the preacher to Christ is founded on the gift of the Holy Spirit. That gift is transmitted and becomes effective through the act of ordination, by work of the Holy Spirit. That it is the Spirit which inspires and impels the messenger of God and brings his revelation to man is testified by both the Old and the New Testaments. It is the Spirit that brought to completion the definitive formulation of the testimonies of faith in the revealed texts; it is the Spirit that accompanies the new interpretation of the texts of the Bible itself and the always indispensable actualization of the Gospel message through preaching. Expertise and human wisdom do not suffice; what is required of the preacher is to inspire and deepen faith, in such a way that man's eternal salvation is effected.

Theses on "Lay Preaching"

The problems posed by the participation of the laity in the official preaching of the Church can be summed up synthetically in the following theses:

1. Being a Christian brings with it the obligation to testify to the faith in the world and in the Church. This witness is demanded of every Christian in everyday life. The sacraments of Baptism and Confirmation qualify us for this action and also impose on us the obligation to bear witness. However, this qualification itself does not suffice to bestow or remove the task of preaching during divine service, even if it were to be granted by ecclesial authority. Nor can the authorization of the individual to preach during the Eucharist, i.e., to give the homily, be deduced from the responsibility of the whole Christian community for the transmission of the Gospel.

2. The mission to preach, and qualification for it, entail a specific preparation of the preacher with the infusion of the Holy Spirit. This spiritual empowerment among Christians can be grounded in personal and individual charism, such as to qualify them through this charism to assume a canonical mission to preach in particular circumstances. Consequently,

specialized expertise, or particular experiences, either of a general or spiritual kind, can provide a sufficient basis for laypeople to give their testimony on individual themes even during the celebration of the Eucharist.

3. Charism as such, however, is both specific and also unstable. It is distinguished both by qualification for a clearly delimited sphere of action and the temporary or provisional nature of such qualification. In that respect, a charism conceived in the biblical sense cannot substitute for a ministerial qualification to preach. For such qualification is not provisional, nor is it temporary: it implies giving official instruction to the community on diverse matters and in a lasting manner. That is why the Church has the responsibility to ensure the spiritual qualification of the preacher in respect to all decisive preaching on faith and salvation.

4. The Church as social body has its juridical order rooted in her sacramental structure, in contrast to other groups. The Church's canonical and sacramental acts are consequently two inseparably interwoven but not identical realities. What happens at the level of canon law cannot therefore be equated with what happens at the level of grace in the sacrament. The gift of the Spirit necessary to be able to preach is not, and cannot be, granted by episcopal delegation to preach. Such delegation should therefore be seen not as a sacramental but as a canonical act: assignment of a pastoral area and authorization to preach.

5. Service to the Gospel is founded in a particular grace, also according to Vatican II. It should be understood as a specific relationship of the ordained minister to Christ, which permits "ministerial action in the person of Christ the Head." It is the Spirit granted by ordination that creates this special relationship to Christ. So ordination must be regarded as the real and unconditional act of qualification to preach. For all those who would like to enter into the service of preaching the Gospel, another alternative is available in the Church: ordination to the diaconate.

THE HERMENEUTIC HORIZON

Whoever agrees with the theological elucidation of so-called "lay preaching" presented here may conclude that the Council only brought confusion to the service of the Church; it would have been better to leave everything as it was before. Yet the aim here is not to confuse nor to preserve the *status quo* nor simply to deny to the laity any opportunity to preach. Our reflections are aimed, instead, at preventing a pragmatic attitude from leading to theologically untenable consequences. For the appointment of the non-ordained to the Church's preaching service as such encounters serious theological obstacles. To ignore these would fundamentally damage the role of the ordained ministry, in the way conceived and defined by Vatican II.

Unity of Services of the Church's Ministry

In his first encyclical *Deus Caritas Est* Pope Benedict XVI teaches: "The Church's deepest nature is expressed in her threefold responsibility: of proclaiming the word of God (*kerygma-martyria*), celebrating the liturgy (*leitourgia*), and exercising the ministry of charity (*diakonia*). These duties presuppose one another and are inseparable" (no. 25). Just this inseparability of ministerial duties would make questionable any mandate to preach that is independent of the assignment of priests to the celebration of the liturgy (*leiturgia*) and to pastoral service (*diakonia*), for it would separate the threefold field of activity of the ministry and institutionalize individual services as separate spheres of activity. Any attempt to compartmentalize, or "privatize," as it were, the appointment to preach, remove it from the Church's threefold responsibility, and thus separate it from the service of sanctification and governance in the Church, is fraught with problems. And these problems are especially apparent in the light of the Eternal High Priest.

The interpretation of the life and ministry of Jesus by the New Testament, and also by the early Fathers of the Church and the Catholic tradition as a whole,[2] teaches that in Christ the

[2] See in particular Paul Dabin, *Le sacerdoce royal des fidèles*, Brüssel, 1950.

eschatological prophet, priest, and pastor came in a single person. So, in the action of Christ the threefold action through which God accomplishes salvation in the Church and in the world—the fields of preaching, liturgical celebration, and charity—cannot be separated from one another. It follows that Christ's model ought also to characterize the structure and ministry through which the Church's salvific mission is accomplished. In addition, the inseparability of the three functions (e.g., the relationship between Word and Sacrament, unifying government and Eucharist, etc.), and their interpenetration in theology, would also preclude their separate institutionalization.

Spiritual Dimension of the Church's Action

No one doubts that many non-ordained members of the Church have better know-how and better experience of life in many fields. Theology itself owes so much to the efforts of laypeople who have devoted themselves to it with great intensity and with outstanding success. The rhetorical ability of philologists, jurists, or the politically engaged would also surely be far greater than that of many ordained ministers. Nor can it be our goal to suggest that these qualities are, supernaturally considered, inconsequential. But can they be the decisive factor, when—in a borderline case—natural intelligence and spiritual qualification interact?

It should almost be considered a foregone conclusion that a preacher, conscious of all the consequences of his sermon, would never dare to rely only on his own self-confidence and do without a sacrament specifically instituted in the Church so that the Church's salvific service would be supported by God's assistance and thus become as fruitful as possible.

Identification with the Church

The reasons that lead individuals to study theology are many. For the most part they are mixed and interact with one another. The pursuit of knowledge as an end in itself can be a source of interest; personal questions of faith can move one; service to man's quest for salvation can make its claim; and the wish for a credible testimony can make us recognize the need for theological reflection on it. In some cases the wish to become involved in this concrete, and sometimes also conflicted, Church will also be a motive for theological study.

The accord between theology and Church is on the whole tacit. Much of what is reported in the media is exaggerated: it leads public opinion to infer that disharmony between theologians and ministers in the Church is normal, even necessary. Despite that, the power of conviction of the Gospel is still closely dependent on the credibility of the Church, and the effort to make these two aspects coincide cannot be avoided. That is why the Gospel still needs today individuals who are profoundly rooted in the Church, who wish to stand with both feet firmly planted on the ground of the Church, and who do not convey the impression that they want to have room for maneuver, in order to gain momentum for a leap into a less controversial area. This total engagement in the Church is realized through ordination, which creates a close bond with the Lord and with his Church. This bond cannot be broken. Nor can it be shaken by a critical look at the errors and defects of the Church. It is the essential premise of preaching: it enhances and strengthens our ability to bear witness in it.

REVIVAL OF THE TRIDENTINE CONCEPTION OF THE PRIEST?

The liturgical and ritual activity of religions and of the Old Covenant experienced a radical modification through Jesus Christ. The concept of priest was especially affected by this. For through Christ its confinement to a liturgical or ritual dimension was avoided: it was opened by the Spirit to a far wider horizon. It is not the performance of sacrifice or the celebration of a rite, but God's election that turns the person called into a New Testament priest; the action of the priest is not limited to worship in church, but extends to and involves daily life, humanity, and the cosmos. And it was Vatican II which in its Decree on the Ministry and

Life of Priests (*Presbyterorum Ordinis*) incorporated the mission of worship in the threefold nature of the ministry of priests: Priests as Ministers of God's Word (*PO* 4), Priests as Ministers of the Sacraments and the Eucharist (*PO* 5), and Priests as Rulers of God's People (*PO* 6). Only when they work in reciprocity, when their interpenetration is achieved, do all three functions of the priest become truly clear.

Yet when we inquire into the fundamental characteristic that binds all three ministries together, we find it in the central significance of the ministry of the Word. According to Joseph Ratzinger, the conciliar texts affirm, without the shadow of a doubt, "that the Word, grasped in all its depth, is the fundamental aspect and constantly comprises the other two ministries (i.e., sanctification and rule) that spring from it and that operate as the two articulations of its reality."[3]

It is well known that the Council of Trent powerfully emphasized the liturgical task of the ordained minister in the Church. It felt it had to take a stance against Luther's repudiation of the Sacrament of Holy Orders (Luther: "This sacrament was invented by the Church of the Pope") and to correct his reduction of the priest's service to the preaching of the Word ("We teach through the Word, we transubstantiate through the Word, we sacrifice through the Word . . ."). This massive attack mounted by Luther understandably narrowed the view of the Council fathers. During Vatican II, after long discussions, it proved possible to supplement the Tridentine view of the priest and to enunciate its biblical contours. What a setback it would be, what a retreat to a one-sided and obsolete theology, if today the integral profile of the ordained presbyter and its grounding in the Sacrament of Ordination were to be sacrificed for the "pottage" of lay preaching!

---

[3] On the question of the meaning of the ordained ministry of the priest: *Geist und Leben* 41 (1968), 347–376.

9

"SACERDOS ALTER CHRISTUS"—THE PRIEST AS "ANOTHER" CHRIST?

With regard to what happens in Baptism, Saint Paul explicitly uses the image of clothing: "For as many of you as were baptized into Christ have put on Christ" (Gal 3:27). This is what is fulfilled in Baptism: we put on Christ, he gives us his garments and those are not something external. It means that we enter into an existential communion with him, that his being and our being merge, penetrate one another. "It is no longer I who live, but Christ who lives in me," is how Paul himself describes the event of his Baptism in his Letter to the Galatians (2:20). Christ has put on our clothes: the pain and joy of being a man, hunger, thirst, weariness, our hopes and disappointments, our fear of death, all our apprehensions until death. And he has given to us his "garments." What in the Letter to the Galatians Paul describes as a simple "fact" of Baptism—the gift of new being—he presents to us in the Letter to the Ephesians as an ongoing task: "Put off your old nature which belongs to your former manner of life . . . and put on the new nature, created after the likeness of God in true righteousness and holiness. Therefore, putting away falsehood, let everyone speak the truth with his neighbor, for we are members of one another. Be angry but do not sin . . ." (Eph 4:22–26).

This theology of Baptism returns in a new way and with a new insistence in priestly ordination. Just as in Baptism an "exchange of clothing" is given, so also in priesthood there is an exchange:

in the administration of the sacraments, the priest now acts and speaks "*in persona Christi.*" In the sacred mysteries, he does not represent himself and does not speak expressing himself, but speaks for the Other, for Christ. Thus, in the sacraments, he dramatically renders visible what being a priest means in general; what we have expressed with our *Adsum*—I am ready, during our consecration to the priesthood: I am here so that you may make use of me. We put ourselves at the disposal of the One who "died for all, that those who live might live no longer for themselves . . ." (2 Cor 5:15). Putting ourselves at Christ's disposal means that we allow ourselves to be attracted within his 'for all': in being with him we can truly be "for all."

— *Pope Benedict XVI, Homily during the Chrism Mass,*
Saint Peter's Basilica, Holy Thursday, April 5, 2007

VATICAN II'S AIDS TOWARDS AN UNDERSTANDING

The rich fruits of the last Council can in no way be considered harvested. Not least is that the case for the Decree on the Ministry and Life of Priests (*Presbyterorum Ordinis*). The Council fathers worked long and intensively on its drafting. This is shown by the fact that the first draft prepared by the preparatory commission (*Antepraeparatoria*) on the theme "priests" went through seven different versions. During the various stages of the decree's genesis a total of over 2,200 proposed improvements were suggested by the bishops, either presented in writing to the editorial committee or read out *viva voce* in the conciliar chamber.

We need not consider here the study of the editorial history of the text is so important for an appropriate interpretation of the final version. It needs no justification: anyone familiar with the historical and critical methods of exegesis, will certainly approach the analysis of a text on the basis of the editorial alterations it has undergone and the historical background of its individual statements. Not all the interesting aspects of the conciliar idea of the priest can be gone into here. The present focus is instead upon one of the many questions about the genesis of the text of the decree: i.e., how it seeks to describe in greater detail the nature of the ordained minister's relationship to Christ. The understanding of ministry in the Church is determined not least by the belief that Christ the Lord is himself at work in the priest's action and in this way sanctifies it. How does Vatican II interpret this relationship to Christ? A short historical excursus may help.

ÉCOLE FRANÇAISE

Pierre de Berulle († 1629), Charles de Condren († 1641), and Jean Jacques J. Olier († 1657) helped foster an inner renewal of the French clergy. Their thoughts and ideas on the renewal of the priesthood were first disseminated in a major publication in which Father Métézeau[1] described the dignity and honor of the priesthood. This book was invaluable for the renewal of the priestly mission. Especially the Society of Saint Sulpice, an order born from the apostolate of Olier that aimed to serve those preparing for ordination to the presbyteral ministry, responded to its appeal and turned it into the focal point of its mission. The society has for over 300 years helped form the rectors of seminaries in many countries and powerfully spread the idea of priestly holiness.

According to Father Métézeau, the priest is distinguished—irrespective of his activity—by an intrinsic holiness. He is interpreted as an *alter Christus*, as another Christ here on earth. "The priest must be a likeness of Christ; he is so by virtue of his state; he is so thanks to the 'indelible mark' (*character indelebilis*), the authority and grace of his ordination." In his exposition of the lofty status of the ministerial priesthood, J.J. Olier went so far as to exclaim: "O incomparable elevation of the priest, who

---

[1] Paul Métézeau, *De sancto sacerdotio, eius dignitate et functionibus sacris* . . . . Paris, 1631.

like a resurrected Jesus Christ realizes everything in the Church with supreme authority. [...] Saint John the Evangelist says of the Word that 'all things were made through him, and without him nothing was made that was made' (Jn 1: 3). Could one not say the same of the priest for everything that is made in the Church? For he is the source of all the good that is done there, and without him no grace would be communicated to man."[2] In this quotation the priest's identity with Christ is made absolute. He represents Christ—*tout court* and without distinctions of any kind.

However, these words should not be understood as statements of systematic theology: the masters of the *École française* had no intention of presenting a systematic theological study of the priesthood. Their aim, in all their treatments, was hortatory rather than dogmatic: to intensify the striving for priestly perfection. Their positive effect on priests was also considerable, as the judgment of the history of the Church has confirmed. Despite that, it did have some problematic consequences.

One is the emphasis they placed on the individualization of the priest. The communal basis of his existence, as enunciated in the theological truth of the *presbyterium*, and his bond with the bishop are correspondingly weakened or obscured. According to the *École française*, the priest, by both formation and consecration, is armed for single combat. He is a warrior who stands alone. He is the man consecrated to God, the witness of the eternal. Separated from the community, he is placed in a different dimension, and confronts society (as it were) from outside. The high claims made for him can hardly be satisfied by life. Yet this glorification of the priest proved resilient: it had a long life. That the priest was to be identified *tout court* with Christ can still be felt in the papal encyclicals of the last century, as can be exemplified by the teachings of both Popes Pius XI and Pius XII.

---

[2] Cited after I. Noye, 'Sacerdoce et sainteté d'après le P. Métézeau,' in *La tradition sacramentale*, edited by the Faculté Théologique de Lyon, Le Puy, 1959, 169–189.

PRIEST AS *ALTER CHRISTUS* IN PRECONCILIAL ENCYCLICALS

Pius XI affirmed in his encyclical on the Catholic priesthood *Ad catholici sacerdotii* (1935): "Priests have a duty which, in a certain way, is higher than that of the most pure spirits 'who stand before the Lord.' Is it not right, then, that he live an all but angelic life?" (no. 45). For Pius XI the fundamental requirement for the ordained minister is his salvific service: he therefore calls the pres-byter the "minister of Christ." He describes the relationship of the ordained minister to Christ as follows: "Thus the priest, as is said with good reason, is indeed 'another Christ'; for, in some way, he is himself a continuation of Christ" (no. 12): he makes Christ present.[3] So the presbyter's unlimited representation of Christ is expressed by the formula *sacerdos alter Christus*. Pius XII writes in a similar way that priests should be "free of all sins . . . adorned with outstanding virtues . . . the height of holiness . . . [in order] to communicate to all men the supernatural light of God and the supernatural life" (*Menti nostrae*, 1950). The same Pope teaches in his encyclical on the sacred liturgy *Mediator Dei* (1947) that prior to acting as representative of the community, "the priest is the ambassador of the divine Redeemer. He is God's vice-gerent (*personam gerit Domini nostri*) in the midst of his flock precisely because Jesus Christ is Head of that body of which Christians are members" (no. 40).

Closer examination of these encyclicals will show that they describe the *being* of the priest. The relationship of the ordained minister with Christ determines, even substitutes for, his own being. It would thereafter make of him a specific presence of Christ, a presence that is conceived as static and continuous. That this presence should be considered a permanent reality is tellingly shown by the way Pope Pius XII, in his encyclical *Mediator Dei*, appeals to the witness of Saint Robert Bellarmine. He refers to him with a quotation which in its original context names Christ,

---

[3] Cf. DS 3755.

the Church, and the presbyters as those who jointly perform the offering of Mass. Bellarmines's intention was to describe the subjects who act during the celebration and not the being that precedes them. And in his analysis he does not fail to limit the theological definition of the priest in a twofold way. The original of the passage cited in the encyclical reads: So Christ sacrifices by means of what is lower to him, the Church by means of what is higher: namely, Jesus. "The priest, *inasmuch as he is the one who offers the sacrifice*, is higher than the people and is the servant not of the Church but of Christ, the original mediator."[4] In Pius XII's encyclical, in contrast to Bellarmine's, this exclusive interest in the liturgical act is assigned second place, since his attention is primarily focused on the ontological premises that are the foundation of the priest's action. The consequences run the risk of overinterpreting or distorting the original text.

SYSTEMATIC AND SPIRITUAL PREMISES OF THE CONCILIAR DECREE *PRESBYTERORUM ORDINIS*

The interpretation of the ordained minister and the presence of Christ in him just described was examined at an early stage in the drafting of the Decree on the Ministry and Life of Priests. The expression "representing Christ" (*Christum gerere* or *Christus repraesentare*) was used to describe the priest's role. From the answer given to an objection raised by one Council Father, which was rejected, we can infer how the editorial committee interpreted this formula: the term *Christum repraesentare* is considered appropriate for the ordained minister and was not therefore eliminated from the text, for in the Church's tradition the *sacerdos* is frequently described as "image, type, figure, etc. (*imago, typus, figura*, etc.)" of the High Priest Christ. From this answer, and from its equating of these terms, we are led to the conclusion that the

---

[4] *Controversiarum de sacramento Eucharistiae* . . . . Paris, 1873; the italics are mine.

presbyter's duty to make Christ present is conceived as lasting and constant. So, a continuous ministerially specific presence of Christ distinguishes the presbyter, even independently of his service.

The corrections and proposed improvements offered, for instance, by Cardinal Döpfner of Munich clearly took quite a different view. They questioned the expression "presbyter's own holiness." Instead, they traced back the presbyter's relationship to Christ to a *configuratio*, a configuring to Christ that takes place in the act of ordination itself; the biblical expression "becoming like him" (cf. Phil 3:10, 21) is cited to describe the nature of this configuration. Not least, they objected to the idea that the priest is—in a nutshell—Christ's representative on earth.

In response to an objection made by several bishops, the idea of *mission* was then incorporated into a new draft of the description of the presbyter. Recognition of the mission given to the Church through Christ was used to clarify the dogmatic foundations of the ordained minister: the static conception of the presence of Christ in him thus takes on a dynamic character; it becomes something dynamic; and a presence of Christ in the priest that is specific to his ministry is applied more widely to his action and service. The separation between "sacred" and "profane," typical of the history of religions, is abandoned in favor of an impulse of Christian incarnation in the world.

It goes without saying that a specific marking of the ordained minister by Christ is not fundamentally repudiated, or even weakened, by this change. For such a configuration to Christ can already be deduced from some verses of the apostle to the Gentiles (cf. 2 Cor 5:14ff.). It plays an important role especially for the idea of service in the Church.[5] It also crops up in the enunciation of the Reformation theology of ministry. So, for example, Luther declares in his Merseburg Sermons: "Now when you listen to me, who am a preacher, and listen to me in just the same way as you listen to another person, then you will believe my words in no

---

[5] Cf. Per Erik Persson, *'Repraesentatio Christi.' Der Amtsbegriff in der neueren römisch-katholischen Theologie.* Göttingen, 1966.

other way than you would believe the words of other men. In this way you are damned with me. . . . So you ought not to listen to me as a man who preaches the words of men; if you were to listen to me in this way, it would be far better if you were not to listen to me at all. You ought not to listen to your parish priest, therefore, as a man who speaks and preaches the words of men. You should listen to him, instead, as one who speaks the Word out of the mouth of babes and sucklings" [cf. Mt 21:16].[6] For Karl Barth, too, the presence of Christ in the ordained minister is incontrovertible. He treats it in connection with his explanation of the meaning of the title *Vicarius Christi*, though this is a title he primarily applies to bishops.[7]

This presence of Christ in the presbyter, however, is no static or objective presence. The New Testament references to the mission of the Church show it to be dynamic; it is an active presence expressed by the presbyter's mission, his sending forth. It follows, therefore, that the term *Christum repraesentare* or its synonym *personam Christi gerere* is inappropriate.

The Meaning of the Term Repraesentatio *or* Repraesentare

In classical Latin the verb *repraesentare* means "to make" in the sense of presenting or representing (in a visual form or image). The noun *repraesentatio* has the same connotation: it means making present in a visual image or likeness. As Hans Georg Gadamer explains, *repraesentatio* then underwent a shift and took on a quite new meaning "in the light of the Christian conception of the incarnation and the *corpus mysticum*": it took on a juridical meaning as a fully legitimized "representation," and a sacramental and canonical meaning as an "acting as deputy." "The word can clearly take on this connotation—says Gadamer—because the person represented is himself present in the representation." The verb *repraesentare* consequently means, in its profoundest

---

[6] Martin Luther, *Opera omnia.* Weimar Edition (WA), 51,15.
[7] Karl Barth, *Die kirchliche Dogmatik* I/1. Zürich: Zolliko, 7th edition, 1955, 99.

connotation, "to make present [*Gegenwärtigseinlassen*]. ... The crux of the juridical term of representation is that the *persona repraesentata* is only a likeness and representation, and yet the representative, who exercises the rights that derive from the *persona repraesentata*, is dependent on him."[8]

Gadamer's interpretation can be confirmed by some texts of the Latin Church Fathers. In them the "making present" expressed by the term *repraesentare* must be understood in so concrete and unambiguous a way that the act of "making present" must be considered synonymous with "deputizing," "acting in the person of someone else" in the full sense.[9] The platonic scheme of idea and object, original image and its reproduced image, which suggests that *repraesentare* or *repraesentatio* is synonymous with reproduction or visual representation, is therefore inadequate for understanding the term in a Christian context, because what is made present and what comes to assume a concrete reality is no longer limited by its relationship with what is represented, though it remains dependent on it.

The difference between representing Christ, on the one hand, and acting in the person of Christ, on the other, is admittedly subtle, but it is crucial. In the first case, what is described is the once-and-for-all act of "*being made present*": the particular relationship between the representative and the represented is not limited to particular times or activities; it is permanent. The original image so influences, so penetrates, the person who represents it as to make it constantly present in him. So, in this case, the representation is not limited to expressing a contingent event or an intermittent presence of the divine in the representative, but defines a permanent representation, whose presence transcends the brief duration of an individual action and could be interpreted as a "quasi-identity."

---

[8] Hans-Georg Gadamer, *Wahrheit und Methode*. Tübingen, 2nd edition 1965, here 134, note 2 and postscript 476.

[9] Cf. Albert Blaise, art. *repraesentatio: Dictionnaire latin-français des auteurs chrétiens*. Strasbourg, 1954, 714.

In contrast to this, the expression "acting in the person of Christ (*in persona Christi*)" is characterized not by immutability but by mutation. The locution *ex* or *in persona* is inherently distinguished by discontinuity and change. This formula was coined by the early Church Fathers in their prosopographic exegesis. They wanted to express in their biblical commentaries how different persons could come to speak through a single speaker[10] and thus explain how the words of Scripture pronounced by him were not his own but had been put into his mouth by someone else.

The person who is present in the words of the speaker is therefore not present in a permanent manner and does not establish with him a lasting or indissoluble bond. The presence of the *persona repraesentata* in the person who represents him must be limited instead to the time of the speaker or to the actions that express his state of being deputized. Only such an interpretation conforms to the real purpose of the formula *ex* or *in persona:* for it was coined with the aim of describing or underlining the dimension of faith in its exterior manifestation and, at the same time, guaranteeing the theocentric character of the event. It is aimed not at enhancing the position of the representative, but at expressing his subsidiary ministerial incorporation in God's plan of salvation.

So, to return to our initial question about the nature of the ordained minister's relationship to Christ, we can deduce that the active presence of Christ in the presbyter is not to be conceived or formulated with the term *repraesentare*; for it means in its early Christian connotation that the priest should represent, act as deputy for, and make comprehensively present within him another person. The only interpretation that can be considered valid is that of the prosopographic exegesis of the early Church

---

[10] Cf. C. Andresen, 'Zur Entstehung und Geschichte des trinitarischen Personenbegriffs,' in *ZNW* 52 (1961) 1–39. The analysis presented here is confirmed by Joseph Ratzinger, 'Zum Personverständnis in der Dogmatik,' in: J. Speck (ed.), *Das Personverständnis in der Pädagogik und ihren Nachbarwissenschaften*, Münster, 1966, 157–171. See further Siegmund Schlossmann, *Persona und Prosōpou in Recht und christlichem Dogma*, Darmstadt, 2nd edition 1968.

Fathers, which then led in Vatican II to the expression "acting *in persona Christi*" adopted by the Council (cf. *PO* 2).

The idea of speaking through the person of someone else is not only patristic: it was subsequently used by medieval theologians, initially to shed light upon the eucharistic event: in this way they could make it clear that the words spoken in the consecration are the words of Christ himself who is present. Thomas Aquinas († 1274) expanded this insight in his theological reflections on the sacraments and especially on the *sacerdos,* so that the character of acting *in persona Christi* referred not only to the act of consecration, but to the whole of the priest's ministerial activity. We ought not to ignore the fact, however, that such a presence of Christ in the ordained minister cannot be manifested independently of the pastoral activity he performs. In the theology of Saint Thomas, for example, it is always the speech and action of the priest in his administration of the sacraments and in his rule of the community that is the premise and point of departure for affirmations of this kind.[11]

The difference I have attempted to clarify in these reflections between the concept of *alter Christus,* applicable to all the baptized, and the specific faculty to act in the person of Christ, will perhaps help to throw new light on a courageous experiment carried out in the French Church in the 1940s and 1950s that proved to be extremely influential.

Worker Priests

The origins of the worker priest experiment can doubtless be traced back to the recognition of the sterile gulf between baptized and ordained in the Church.[12] According to perceptive observers, this gulf had been widened by the loss of faith of a large part of the French population; this was especially apparent among the French working class in the first half of the last century. In the opinion of many priests, only a concerted "mission" among their

---

[11] Cf. (for example) Thomas Aquinas, *S. Th.* I–II q. 100. a. 8 ; II–III, q. 88, a. 12, C.

[12] Cf. some dubious theses of the *École française.*

working compatriots could make good this loss of faith. The Dominican Jacques Loew began the experiment as a dockworker in Marseilles in 1941.

The love of worker priests for their fellowmen was exemplary, their faith in the Gospel as source of salvation extraordinary, and their heroism in the face of adversity admirable. Yet the experiment also had a tragic side. Though pioneers of the apostolate had already been at work among the laity of Catholic Action, priests were still needed to form the vanguard.

It goes without saying that the "merely" baptized were also involved in the experiment—Henri Perrin, another pioneer of the mission among workers, repeatedly mentions them in his diary. But clearly it was reserved for the priest to make Christ present in this world. Father Perrin thus writes in his diaries: ". . . it's not only the Christian, but especially the priest, that the world must have before its eyes. The world must be able, so to say, to grasp hold of him with its hands. Apparently everything has conspired to isolate us, to cut us off from any genuine contact with the people entrusted to us. Even within the Church there were those who strove to keep the priest far apart from the chance to do anything."[13] And the "green book," in which the worker priests of Paris tried to explain their position to the cardinal of the diocese, Feltin, declares: "If we are priests and workers today, the question is inevitably and unconditionally raised of our priesthood in relation to the Church. We went into the factories, encouraged, even sent, by the Church, in order to give an answer to the absence of Christ among millions of proletarians."[14] And at the end of his diary Father Perrin comments on his undoubtedly courageous commitment: ". . . only the priest can win back certain wholly de-Christianized layers of the population for Christ."[15]

---

[13] Henri Perrin, *Journal d'un prêtre ouvrier en Allemagne* (1945); idem, *Priest and Worker. The Autobiography of Henri Perrin*, translated by Bernard Wall. London: Macmillan, 1965. Perrin's journal is cited here after the German translation: *Tagebuch eines Arbeiterpriesters*, München, 2nd edition, 1956, 351.

[14] Gregor Siefer, *Die Mission der Arbeiterpriester. Ereignisse und Konsequenzen*. Essen, 1960, 80f.

[15] Henri Perrin, op. cit. 352.

How good it is that Vatican II reaffirmed, and placed in view once again, the presence of Christ in every baptized person! The Council did so, first, because this teaching is founded in the words of Holy Scripture. It also had the merit of removing the ordained priest from his burden of isolation and of placing him firmly in the community of the mystical Body of Christ. Further, it clarified the meaning of the common and often repeated expression *sacerdos alter Christus* and in some sense corrected it. Understandably, reflection, revision, and change from habitual trains of thought did not happen without a struggle.

THE NEW TEACHING OF VATICAN II

The presence of Christ—as repeatedly pointed out by the Council—is not something exclusively given to the priest and denied to the other members of the Church. This is the teaching of the baptismal theology of the apostle Paul. He writes, for example, to the Christian community in Galatia: "'For as many of you as were baptized into Christ have put on Christ" (3:27). In using the image of putting on Christ, Paul's purpose was to express what happens in baptism: namely, the beginning of the participation in the being of Christ himself, the birth of another self, the Christ within me, the new man. This new man is already created by God and the old man crucified with Christ in baptism. This is just one of the many statements of the apostle to the Gentiles on the community of Christ, which for every baptized person springs from the sacrament. "I have been crucified with Christ: it is no longer I who live, but Christ who lives in me" (Gal 2:20).

Thus Vatican II adopted an idea from New Testament revelation, in speaking of "living union with Christ" (Decree on the Apostolate of Lay People [*Apostolicam Actuositatem*], no. 4). And the Decree on the Ministry and Life of Priests (*Presbyterorum Ordinis*) affirms, even before its teachings on the priestly ministry: "Therefore there is no such thing as a member that has not a share in the mission of the whole Body. Rather, every single member ought to reverence Jesus in his heart and by the spirit of prophecy give testimony of Jesus" (*PO* 2). Similarly, the Council's Constitution on the Church *Lumen Gentium* speaks of the laity as all those "who by Baptism are incorporated into Christ" and "in their own way share the priestly, prophetic and kingly office of Christ" (*LG* 31).

The "splendid isolation" of the ordained minister from the rest of the baptized that had been fostered by the *École française*, and the high estimation of the priest aspired to by this school, risked a kind of exaltation of the priest. This might have represented, on the one hand, an incentive for the priest and would undoubtedly have increased his attraction; the moving novels of someone like the great Georges Bernanos, which often revolve around the lives of priests, could not have been imagined without it. On the other hand, the powerful searchlight fixed on the priest might have had the collateral effect of obscuring the incorporation of Christ in each and every baptized person. Uniqueness cannot by definition be shared. And other fundamental truths of the faith are also necessarily overshadowed by an exaggerated glorification of the priest; perhaps they were also obscured even in those initiatives that rocked the Church in France in the 1950s and that saw priests directly engaged on the factory floor. It is clear enough that "the experiment and tragedy of worker priests" also had roots in the isolation of the ordained from the community to which they belong and in a one-sided theology of priesthood.

SERVING CHRIST'S PRESENCE IN EVERY BAPTIZED PERSON

Our brief review of the concept of *sacerdos alter Christus* has helped to underline that the ordained minister's relationship to Christ can hardly be described as *repraesentatio* in any absolute or unconditional sense; were that not so, the misunderstanding of the priest's "quasi-identity" with Christ would not be dispelled.

The idea of a specific, static, and objective presence of Christ in the priest would indeed enhance his image, but it would attribute to the ordained a dignity that would ultimately overshadow that of the Lord himself and contradict the equal proximity of all the baptized to God. Moreover it would ignore the character of service of the ordained ministry and be incompatible with the important apostolic characteristic of the Church reaffirmed by Vatican II.

The final draft of the Decree on the Ministry and Life of Priests (*Presbyterorum Ordinis*) tried in all its formulations to avoid the misunderstanding that the presence of Christ in the priest is to be conceived as a lasting presence. It therefore no longer makes use of the expression *repraesentare* or *repraesentatio*, and, in the passages decisive for its systematic theology, no longer mentions a presence of Christ in the presbyter in its erroneous sense of being a unique privilege for him only. Instead it affirms that priests are, by the special character granted by ordination, "able to act in the person of Christ the head" (*PO* 2).

If we interpret this latter phrase in its conciliar context, that of the Decree on the Ministry and Life of Priests, we can, in sum, identify the following features of the priest's relationship to Christ:

1. A term (*repraesentare*) adopted in the early Church and long used in the formulation of the truths of the faith is now out of date and no longer necessarily the best suited from a theological point of view. However, in this as in many other cases, we can assume it comes very close to what is meant by the matter in hand, because it expresses better the significance attributed to it by those closest to its normative origin.

2. The term "acting in the person of Christ (*in persona Christi*)" is now applied to the action of the priest. It therefore expresses the concrete form of the ordained ministry in which the presbyter performs his service (*ministerium*). That such action is characterized by particular "qualities" peculiar

to the *being* of the presbyter ("special character," "seal of the sacrament") has already been amply discussed in Chapter 2.

3. By the addition of the prepositional phrase "in the person of Christ (*in persona Christi*)" the action of the presbyter is placed in a new and theologically crucial dimension of the faith. The previous determination of such action at the level of his immanent ministerial activities is thereby in no way superseded. On the contrary, this addendum at the phenomenological level enables us to perceive the intrinsic meaning of every sign. But such action occurs in our case *in persona Christi*, and the sign is thus given a new importance; it assumes a new value: the ministerial work of the presbyter becomes *sacramental*, i.e., it becomes a sign of salvation: it refers to Christ's work of redemption.

    Christ's salvific action is thus made present: it is made tangible in a specific place and time and—if it be accepted by the faithful—can also have a salvific effect. It is only in the name of Christ, only by acting *in persona Christi*, that the basis of the presbyter's action becomes clear. Neither the natural ability of its bearer, nor appointment and empowerment by the Church, must obscure that it is Christ who makes the presbyter's action effective; it is in Christ that the unique and irreplaceable competence of the presbyter lies.

4. Here we recur to the Augustinian conception according to which Christ is the real source of authority. It is Christ who acts through him, while the presbyter is only given a role of service (*ministerium*). This insight into the priest's subservient role means, on the one hand, the priest's total submission to the sole source of ministerial action, Christ himself, and the recognition that God does not intend to renounce the cooperation and service of man in the history of salvation. On the other hand, this service, according to the biblical model of Christ, is characterized by an unconditional willingness on the part of the priest to serve his fellowmen and

thus to conform to God's will. The twofold claims made of the presbyter as servant necessitate a close bond with Christ, which is institutionally founded and which also influences his existential condition. Thanks to this bond he will try to conform in his spiritual life to the formula *in persona Christi*. For service to Christ cannot be performed in a mechanical or impersonal way. It can only be performed in a deliberate attempt to configure himself to Christ and enter into a relationship at once demanding and enriching. The presbyter in his service to his fellowmen cannot do other than strive to ensure that the sign placed by him, the action he performs in the person of Christ, is believed and accepted by others.[16]

---

[16] Cf. Karl Rahner, *Kirche und Sakramente*. Freiburg, 1960, 2nd edition, 85–95, here in particular 91f.

10

THE PRIEST UNDERSTOOD
IN THE LIGHT
OF SECULAR MODELS

The thesis of "ecclesiological relativism" finds its justification in the opinion that the "historical Jesus" himself did not even think of a Church, let alone found one. It followed that the real creation of the Church only arose after the Resurrection as a process of jettisoning its eschatological foundation due to the inescapable sociological needs of its institutionalization. Initially, too, according to this thesis, not even a "catholic" universal Church existed, but only different local churches with different theologies, different ministers, and so forth. So no institutional Church could claim to be a Church of Jesus Christ willed by God himself; and all institutional forms arose from sociological needs and therefore as such are all human creations, which can and even must be subject to radical change in response to new circumstance. In their theological qualities these churches differ from each other at the most in a secondary way, and hence one can say that in all of them or at any rate in many of them the "one Church of Christ" subsists. So the question naturally arises with what right one can, from such a viewpoint, speak at all of a single Church of Christ. The Catholic tradition, in contrast to this view, has adopted another point of departure: she has faith in the Evangelists; she believes them.

—*Cardinal Joseph Ratzinger, Address on the Constitution on the Church*
Lumen Gentium, *35 years after Vatican II, given at the International*
Conference on Vatican Council II promoted by the Committee
of the Great Jubilee of the Year 2000, February 27, 2000

VATICAN II—CAN IT BE MISUNDERSTOOD?

After lengthy discussion, the Second Vatican Council decided to dedicate the second chapter of the Dogmatic Constitution on the Church *Lumen Gentium* to the People of God and the Church as a whole. Precedence was thus given to the People of God, while treatment of the hierarchical structure of the Church and its articulations was relegated to the following chapter (Chapter III). In other words, the fundamental equality of all the redeemed before God was once again placed in its rightful light. Some verses from the First Letter of Peter were cited in support of this teaching and thus became the scriptural passages cited most often in the Council's documents: "But you are a chosen race, a royal priesthood, a holy nation, God's own people. That you may declare the wonderful deeds of him who called you out of darkness into his marvelous light" (2:9).

In the postconciliar period the equality of birth of all God's chosen people has thus taken precedence over all forms of differentiation within the People of God, and has influenced reflection in the Church more powerfully than any other truth. Vatican II speaks of "the faithful who by Baptism are incorporated into Christ, are placed in the People of God, and in their own way share the priestly, prophetic and kingly office of Christ, and to the best of their ability carry on the mission of the whole Christian people in the Church and in the world" (*LG* 31). At the diocesan and parish levels these statements provided a powerful impulse for the cooperation of the laity in the governance of the Church.

QUALIFICATION TO RULE BY ELECTION

There is no question that the Church has often learned, and indeed has been obliged to learn, from the world. The Fathers of Vatican II indeed acknowledged in the Pastoral Constitution on the Church in the Modern World *Gaudium et Spes* that "the

Church too is not unaware how much it has profited from the history and development of mankind" (*GS* 44). The encounter with modern democratic thought thus became an opportunity for the Church; for it favored a growing interest of the faithful in the Church and an enthusiastic involvement of many in it.

The gulf between a Church leadership that assumes responsibility for everything and a "flock" that remains passive was closed—wholly in conformity with the Gospel. For the Word of God wants not only to be passively heard, but actively experienced and spread by those who listen to it. The involvement of the baptized in the transmission of God's Word is therefore no more than obedience to God's Gospel. The apostolate of the laity in this way received a powerful impulse for its mission. Many parishes would today be reduced to a state of total desolation if members of the parish council had not assumed responsibility in them; not to mention their dedication to organization, administration, and sacramental ministry.

Lay participation was not limited to a few committed individuals. The Old and New Testament truth of the "common priesthood of all members of the People of God" encouraged the sharing of responsibility also through structural changes: the participation of all the baptized in the governance of the community was the ideal objective, but in practice it was reduced to the participation of the laity in elected or appointed bodies: the various pastoral and other councils were thus established. Today the non-ordained are involved in the sharing of responsibility at the various levels of the government of the Church: parish, vicariate forane, bishopric, bishops' conference.

The various consultative bodies are of course of different quality, degree, and significance; the parish council is clearly different in degree and importance from the Central Committee of German Catholics. Yet all these bodies have one thing in common: the impulses of the Second Vatican Council led to the establishment of institutions that exerted influence on the leadership of the Church; they led to the ordained sharing their responsibility with the non-ordained. And in the further development of this renewal, new models of government were developed in various Catholic dioceses, as for instance in Switzerland.

As the statute of one Swiss diocese explains, due to "declining resources, especially in the field of personnel," the intensification of ecclesial work with the help of new "pastoral units" is desirable. Purpose of seeking their help is to achieve "a reinforcement and/or reorganization of pastoral care." Pastoral responsibility for such units is commonly allocated to "various persons (e.g., priests, laymen, and laywomen, who would all call themselves "pastors"). The resulting "collaboration of male and female pastors . . . extends to the whole of the Church's service in the community . . . and should be developed through dialogue." Two types of service are particularly emphasized: the "service of the responsible priest and the service of the pastoral team" (which can be performed without the grace of the Sacrament of Ordination).[1]

The postconciliar involvement of all members of the Church sought new forms for pastoral care and a new definition of their role. Everyday experiences, lay institutions, offered models for her structure and fields of endeavor; proven practices of the more widespread associations or even the executive practice of business concerns served as models. They all pursue particular goals and need supervision. Sociology has examined them under the label "leadership."[2] According to sociology, leadership is inseparable from social groups: one or several persons act as representatives of a collective and enjoy authority. On what does the claim to leadership rest? It is assigned by the group to

---

[1] Quotations are taken from the statutes for the "pastoral units" of the diocese of Saint Gallen, accepted by its bishop on November 7, 2002. The innovative reorganization of pastoral service thus introduced set a surprising precedent for spiritual responsibility for communities in matters of personnel. We may cite as an example the pastoral unit of Saint Gallen-City Center where the team leader is a female pastoral assistant, to whom are assigned one parish priest and one deacon. Another example, diocese of Basel, rectorate of Belp: the female community leader is to be a pastoral assistant to whom is assigned: "one parish priest as assistant." Diocese of Chur, pastoral unit of Dielsdorf: community leader a pastoral assistant to whom is assigned one vicar.

[2] On the following see Wilhelm Bernsdorf's article on leadership: "Führung" in W. Bernsdorf (ed.) *Wörterbuch der Soziologie*. Stuttgart, 1969, 313–319.

its leader/leaders (whether by acclamation or election). In associations regulated by statute or those set up for a special purpose, a selection process has often been developed: suitable candidates for leadership roles are selected by a bottom to top selection process in which the list of candidates is gradually narrowed down by successive elimination.

As a consequence of these postconciliar developments, we thus find, alongside the various traditional levels of decision-making and governance in the Church—that of priest, bishop, pope—persons who have come to fill their positions by altogether dissimilar routes of access. Hierarchy, in short, has come to coexist with democracy. On the one hand, there are those who have been assigned to leadership "from above" and who owe their position to the Sacrament of Ordination; and on the other, there are those who come "from below" and who have been chosen by the members of their group. Both forms of legitimation need to be carefully distinguished. Only those who ignore the foundation of the Church in divine grace can attribute the same authority to them all without distinction. Vice versa, whoever recognizes that during the Sacrament of Ordination those specific qualities of the priesthood that are enunciated during its celebration, and cited in the *Traditio apostolica*,[3] are conferred on the ordinand, will not find here the specific task of leadership assigned to the ordained.

Yet more is at stake than the authority of leadership that rests on the Sacrament of Ordination. According to the jurist and later constitutional judge G. Leipholz, it was Christianity and humanism that largely determined traditional Western democratic thought in Europe. Examined more closely, the roots of modern democracy can be traced back to the England of Oliver Cromwell († 1658). The Puritans—the Pilgrim Fathers—left the island and immigrated to North America. They brought with

---

[3] See the rite of ordination described in the Apostolic Tradition of Hippolytus of Rome (*c*.215), prayer to God to "impart the spirit of grace," so that you [the priest] may "protect and guide your people with a pure heart" (no. 7). On the *Traditio apostolica*, see above 39–41.

them democratic thinking regarding the form of their social life. Initially they placed their Covenants, their compacts on how their communities ought to be organized and ruled, expressly under the sovereignty of God. The biblical statements concerning the "common priesthood" were cited to provide justification. When subsequently the people came to participate in the rule of the state and in the administration of power, it marked a step towards secularization: the principles that inspired the form of government were gradually separated from the context of divine revelation. So G. Leipholz argued that the first examples of modern democracy in the Anglo-American world could be found in the "transfer of the spiritual priesthood to all the faithful in a non-theological language."[4] It would be a fatal error if this transfer were to be replicated in the Church, i.e., if a new order were to be conceived in her that squandered the transcendental foundation of her ministry of ruling, and if God, in conformity with the contemporary idea of democracy, were to be dethroned even within the Church, as he has already been dethroned in society.

MAJORITY DECISION OR *COMMUNIO?*

The meaning of being qualified in the mission of the Church is often misunderstood by poorly informed or external observers. Public opinion has been misled into supposing that an absolutist system is here being superseded by a democratic one. Not just those outside the Church draw this conclusion. The members of the new groups that have arisen in the postconciliar period at various levels of the Church have misunderstood the implications of such bodies and developed a false conception of their role. No longer accepting the traditional hierarchical system of superordination and subordination in the Church, they claimed the right to participate in all decisions. They thought the time had come for power in the Church to be newly carved up and

---

[4] Gerhard Leipholz, *Das Wesen der Repräsentation und der Gestaltwandel der Demokratie im 20. Jahrhundert.* Berlin, 1966, 211 ff.

for the Church to be administered according to secular ideas. The Church was interpreted by them as a purely earthly reality. And in some countries efforts were made to express this profane understanding in new structures.

The dioceses of the Federal Republic of Germany, like those elsewhere, responded to the impulses of Vatican II, which were a central theme at the Würzburg Synod (1972–75). This assembly of all the levels of the People of God clearly drew its inspiration from political experiences and hoped for abundant pastoral fruits with the help of parliamentary models. It proposed that the bishops should issue instructions to authorize parish councils to participate in the decision-making process; it further proposed that not the ordained parish priest, by virtue of his ministry, but an elected layperson should chair the parish council. It proposed something similar for the episcopal level, though here the chairmanship of the council would be assigned to the diocesan bishop.

The Code of Canon Law, which Pope John Paul II promulgated on January 25, 1983 and whose observance was made obligatory for the whole Latin Church, rejected these special German regulations. But since this illegal practice continued here and there, a new Decree of the supreme tribunal of the Apostolic Signatura was issued on January 28, 2008. It abrogated particular laws and regulations issued on the basis of local conditions or particular circumstances and explicitly sanctioned the annulment of the instructions approved by the Würzburg Synod.

An attentive ecclesiology can help us to understand this twofold intervention of the Holy See's highest judicial authorities. In conducting such an ecclesiological examination, we must above all avoid the criteria of the secular or worldly logic of power. Only then will we escape the error of supposing that the aim of Vatican II was to democratize the Church or equating ordained and laity in the distribution of power. Whoever would like to force democracy on the Church inevitably sees it from the viewpoint of secular power; for democracy is a constitutional system that serves power (whereas the Church is a sacramental system that serves God). To decide and to act in the Church according to the parliamentary model would therefore be inherently wrong. Nor can there be any autonomy of the laity vis-à-vis the hierarchy, for there exists no sphere in which the laity can assume exclusive responsibility for the world and independently build it up, without at the same time building up the Church.[5]

Undoubtedly the Church's pastors are incorporated in, and form an inseparable part of, the community relationships created within the People of God. Only in their awareness that they are in the first instance baptized like all their fellow-Christians can their judgment be formed. Only then will they particularly take to heart the need to consult with the councils at the various levels of the Church. The Church is no absolutist system ruled by authoritarian instructions or directives. Yet her fundamental decisions are not reached according to the majority principle. She has the task of bearing witness to the faith. Faith, however, is divinely established: its tenets cannot be decided according to political criteria; faith is only integral if it is transformed into life. And instruction in the faith can only take place if the ordained pastor has the last word. The assumption of secular models in the Church is only possible if they are radically transformed and founded anew.

The foundation for the order of the Church is not the parliamentary model, but the life that flows from the sacraments. The Christian is someone who has encountered the Lord in his Word and in his signs: the individual and the community of faith live from the gift of the Holy Spirit. Guided by the Spirit, the Church is shown her way through history. He was promised to the Church by the Lord and "will guide you into all the truth" (Jn 16:13). He infused the disciples of the Lord with the power of witness at Pentecost "so that they were all filled with the Holy Spirit" (Acts 2:1–4). He guided the young Church in choosing

---

[5] Here too, over three decades since it was written, the study of the late Bishop of Lugano, Eugenio Corecco, remains as relevant as ever: 'Kirchliches Parlament oder synodale Diakonie,' in *Ikt* 1 (1972), 33–53.

the apostle Matthias (Acts 1:26). He inspired the decisions of the first council, so that the apostles could say: "It has seemed good to the Holy Spirit and to us to lay upon you no greater burden than these necessary things" (Acts 15:28).

The Holy Spirit is articulated in countlesss ways through the words of each of the baptized. Each Christian has his charism, his gift of the Spirit. That is why each has the right to speak. The responsible pastors are especially bound to listen—they more than others—and not to pass off their own prejudice or caprice, their own stubbornness, as the teaching of the Spirit. They must be sure of the gift of the Spirit in a particular way. For by their appointment to the ministry through ordination they were armed with grace and divine strength, gifts that distinguish them from the non-ordained. The oldest surviving prayer of consecration from the Traditio apostolica (*c.*215) invokes the gift of the Holy Spirit for the bishop: "Impart the spirit of grace and the wisdom of the elders [*presbyterium*], that he may help and guide your people with a pure heart." So the Church prays and believes that the bishop's service will be supported by the promised effects of the sacrament. It is this that distinguishes the rank of the ordained minister from all others called to a mission in the Church. And no one really guided by the Holy Spirit will ever leave this out of account. The Letter to the Hebrews urges not without reason: "Obey your leaders and submit to them; for they are keeping watch over your souls, as men who will have to give account. Let them do this joyfully, and not sadly, for that would be of no advantage to you" (13:17).

At the same time the Holy Spirit is not a Spirit of discord, of factions and parties. His method is not that of the narrow majority decision or the popular vote, familiar to us from the democratic system. He is received by those who congregate "all together in one place" to pray (Acts 2:1). He preserves the community in concord, so that it be "of one heart and soul" (Acts 4:32). Christ's community is thus distinguished by unanimity. Schisms and discord, or the emergence of opposition groups, show that the life of a community is not founded on the precepts and Gospel of Christ (cf. 1 Cor 1:10 ff.).

Consequently, only those can act as faithful members of the Church, who recognize and profess their own belonging to Christ and never forget that their fellow-Christians do likewise, whether they be ordained ministers with their specific endowments for service in the Church or laity. Only in this way can the spiritual reality of the Body of Christ characterize life in the diocese and in the parish. Only thus can decisions be matured and made from the unity of the common Spirit. The multitude of separate voices must again and again be led back to well-tempered harmony as much as possible. The more unified is the formation of opinion in solving a problem, the more likely it is that God's Spirit is at work. For the structure proper to the Church is not parliamentarianism but *communio*.[6]

In the postconciliar Church the word *communio* had all the allure of a new theological discovery. This term turns up again and again and we are assured of the high value attached to it: unity and mutual understanding are among man's basic yearnings. And, besides, the use of the term by the early Fathers of the Church reveals its preciousness.

What is especially striking in the patristic sources is that they all insist on the theocentric origin of *communio*. For instance, Saint Irenaeus of Lyon († *c.*202): according to him the unity of man is God-given and grows from communion with Christ: "The Lord has redeemed us with his blood. He has given us his soul instead of our own, his flesh instead of our own, and he has poured out his Spirit over us, in order to produce unification (*henosis*) and communion (*koinonia*) between God and man."[7] Many similar quotations can be found in the theologians of the early Church.

---

[6] See for instance Cardinal Joseph Ratzinger, "*Communio*—a Program," lecture at the Gregorian University in Rome, May 28, 1992. The present writer has also discussed the concept of *communio* in his book *Communio. Utopie oder Programm*, in the series *Quaestiones disputatae* (no. 148), Freiburg: Herder, 1993.

[7] Irenaeus of Lyon, *Adv. haer.* 4,33,4.

Here is the fundamental reason why decision-making and action in the Church cannot be achieved through the democratic process. The difference between community life according to the ideal of *communio* on the one hand and parliamentarianism, indeed the political world of ideas as a whole, on the other, cannot be ignored. Politics sets itself goals; it pursues objectives. The "striving after participation in power, or after influence in the distribution of power" (Max Weber), belongs to the very nature of politics. When Christians come together, by contrast, they do so in the first place not to make decisions or take action. They are in unity, even before they begin to act; and they do not decide and act as Christians if their action does not reflect the unity that subsists between them. It is no accident that the documents of the Second Vatican Council were discussed for so long, or that countless consecutive drafts of them were produced, until near-unanimity was reached.

It is especially the members of the various councils in the Church who tend, in conformity with their talents or expertise and their idea of responsibility, to engage in debate according to the example of politicians and parliamentarians; that is why they in particular must pay special attention to the basic law of *communio*. There are other reasons why the democratic model cannot be decisive for them. For it corresponds neither to the foundation nor to the sense of their membership of councils: they have been given a consultative role in the Church not because others transferred a portion of power to them by nominating them to serve on a council, but because the community trusts in their intellectual and spiritual endowment—or charism—for the building up of the community. The elected person should bring this personal charism to the council on which he serves and express it through his testimony of faith. Each individual, however, bears witness according to his own faith; so no one can be the representative of someone else's faith, still less saddled with a particular position by a pressure group outside the Church.

FUNCTIONALITY INSTEAD
OF TRANSMISSION OF FAITH

Apart from the influence of political thought, the wish for greater pastoral efficiency has had a powerful influence on Church leaders. There is hardly any German diocese that is not in the process of creating new pastoral structures. The changing demographic pattern of our towns and cities and especially the shortage of priests are cited in justification of such reforms. Business consultants are asked for their advice and bring their expertise; and it goes without saying that they see the Church from the same viewpoint with which they view big business. The identity of priests is especially affected by the new "pastoral units" that have been created in the Church. The shifting of ministerial service from the sacramental to the functional level means that the priest is no longer seen as a witness, but as a "role-player."

There is no doubt that professional profiles, or specialized skills, can improve the Church's pastoral service and the way in which specific activities are performed in the community and in the Church. The priest, whether from inclination or particular expertise, may wish to choose between different spheres of pastoral activity or different target groups: pastoral care in schools, in youth groups, in families, among the elderly or in hospitals. Working plans and curricula need to be formulated to ensure that the particular needs of the target groups are met in a suitable way. Specialization may also be meaningful in particular cases, bearing in mind the various human capacities available for a particular service. The whole spectrum of sociological knowledge needs to be applied to the action of the Church; and this is of no small assistance to all ordained ministers and for the quality of their service.

Max Müller

Yet the fragmentation of professional roles, the dividing up of personnel into specialized vocational sectors, has its limits for ordained ministers. For if functional thought were systematically applied to the various kinds of service in the Church, the end result would inevitably be that the ordained ministry itself would be subordinated to it.

The German philosopher Max Müller discussed the effects of functional thought in his essay "Person und Funktion."[8] His remarks also hold good for ecclesiology. Müller pointed out that the ministry only exists if the universality of the faith in all its dignity and articulations is present in it and in the person who holds it. The ministry "is simultaneously the presence of the universal and the supra-individual in the individual." The ordained minister is therefore, ontologically, more than that which constitutes his work. In a world in which work is segmented and characterized by specialization of roles and the subdivision of tasks, a "ministry," in Müller's view, is no longer realizable. But if the ordained ministry were to disappear, the universal would no longer be present in the community dimension to which we are called; the "supra-individual dimension" would be invisible. In other words: The unconditional acceptance of the functional perspective and its application to service in the Church would destroy the plausibility of the ordained ministry and together with it the chance to encounter what is universal in the Church in her representatives.

Yet the most important reason against imposing professional expertise and specialization in the place of service in the Church lies in the pastoral mission itself. Reliance upon technical skill and methodology brings one into conflict with the anthropological and theological presuppositions inherent in the Church's pastoral ministry. If the sociological view were to be absolutized, the order within the Church would be reduced to an industrial system; it would be secularized. For the model of business consultancy cannot easily grasp the central human factors, still less the spiritual motives, of the Church's ministry.

---

[8] Max Müller, in: *Philosophisches Jahrbuch* 69 (1961/62), 371–404, here 401.

While the reorganization of the pastoral territory may be unavoidable for the administration of pastoral areas or for a diocese, pastoral care itself remains something apart. For pastoral care is ultimately directed not to professional fields, but to the human person. Moreover, the preoccupation with structures corresponds to the business model and is aimed at visible (or quantifiable) success. Thus it may even pose a risk for pastoral care. The preaching of the Gospel and the discovery of God's power in our life spring from other sources. What purpose would Church service propose to realize if these goals were to be renounced?

Far-sighted sociologists themselves underline that the transmission of the faith must transcend the structural and impact on the personal level; territorial and functional reform is not in itself enough. Franz-Xaver Kaufmann thus argues in sociological terms that efforts to spread Christianity today are doomed to failure because too little attention is paid to the "interactive level." But such interaction presupposes personal encounter. "Identification with persons we love or admire is the premise for accepting the values that, in the last analysis, will lead us to embrace Christianity."[9]

Jean Mouroux

The French theologian Jean Mouroux has convincingly described the *personal* character of the act of faith.[10] According to Mouroux, the act of faith demands that the human person respond to the personal God: it "is the response of the human person to the personal God and therefore the meeting of two persons." Will, thought, and spiritual feelings are involved in every meeting between human beings; but the act that determines real communion is the spiritual impetus of the person himself (*l'élan spirituel de la personne même*) to follow someone else; the individual

---

[9] Franz-Xaver Kaufmann, *Kirche begreifen. Analysen und Thesen zur gesellschaftlichen Verfassung des Christentums*. Freiburg, 1979, 18.

[10] Jean Mouroux, *Je crois en Toi*. Paris, 1949; English translation: *I Believe in You: The Personal Structure of Faith* (1938); German edition: *Ich glaube an Dich. Von der personalen Struktur des Glaubens*. Einsiedeln, 1951; the page numbers interpolated in the text refer to the German edition.

is moved and enters into a relationship. It is then that his whole spiritual being is opened. This interpersonal meeting is analogous to the act of faith in which the individual accepts the God who is calling to him. Reason, love, and will react; love will become the gateway to faith (25f.).

Mouroux calls the act of faith "*obscure*" (29). This adjective signifies that by its very nature it escapes scientific evidence; it cannot be reduced to an objective value or to the level of rational critique; it finds its scope in the subjective and individual dimension. The reasons that lead someone to give himself to another person cannot be grasped. All reason can do—so to say, *post factum*—is attempt to fathom the relationship and justify it. But what goes for a deep human attachment to another person goes infinitely more for our relationship to God: the abandonment to God remains all the more obscure because it is determined by the self-revelation of a divine person, which remains hidden by the veil of grace. It follows that it must be mediated by human witness. Moreover, to this is added the fact that the person called by God is a fallen person; the burden of sin that weighs on him additionally blocks his path to God. A painful process of purification is needed; it is the fruit of the Spirit (29–35). Augustine speaks of the "eyes of faith" that are able to see in the light, and of the "hands of faith" that are able to feel in the dark.

That is why the new spiritual movements and communuities in the Church place so much emphasis on the *personal* aspect of faith: they strive towards the central and urgent objective of enabling each Christian in his or her unique individual history to encounter the person of Jesus Christ in the world they inhabit. This need for a personal encounter with the Lord is underlined, for instance, in the well-known publication of the late prior of Taizé, Father Roger Schutz: *The Today of God*. Similarly, another publication, *Contemplation of Life in Community*, is aimed at sharpening the eyes of the members of the spiritual family of Charles de Foucauld to the presence of Christ in their everyday life. Faith must increasingly have today—as Karl Rahner put it—"mystic and contemplative quality" and thus find its raison d'être in unity with the person of Jesus Christ.

Luigi Giussani

The founder of the *Comunione e Liberazione* (Communion and Liberation) movement, Luigi Giussani, a priest and philosopher from Milan, has examined some aspects of *communio* in detail.[11] In his experience, which is now shared by hundreds of thousands of people all over the world, the faith can be newly aroused by the yearning for the Christian event to be reenacted in us today; the yearning for Christ to happen again in our time—for Christ to become a living reality in the daily life that challenges us day by day.

What characterizes such a Christian event? It is expressed in the form of an impulse, a movement, through which the man Jesus of Nazareth, who was born and was killed so long ago, becomes important for the very core of my life. He looks at me through the face of someone living today—through a friend, a companion, through quite ordinary people, in just the same way Jesus did when he looked into the faces of those around him and chose his disciples and sent them out two by two, carrying "no purse, no bag, no sandals," into the villages of Palestine where he himself intended to go. And they experienced that they too were powerful "in his name" (Lk 10). So the Christian event is primarily a human meeting, through which Jesus Christ shows himself to be important for our own heart and in which we are enabled to discover our own identity. The last great rhetorician of the classical world, Gaius Marius Victorinus († 362), declared: "Ever since I met Christ I have discovered myself as a person." Victorinus pronounced these words from the pulpit of the church of Sant'Ambrogio in Milan, 300 years after Christ's death. He had recognized Christ in the faces of the young Christians who could not contain their joy and enthusiasm on hearing of his conversion.

---

[11] Luigi Giussani's books have been published in English editions by McGill-Queen's University Press.

Anyone who encounters Christ in his brother or sister will never be the same again: the experience will change his life. Only by this personal encounter with Christ in our fellowmen can Christianity obtain new existential relevance for us. The heart of our life will be moved by hitherto unknown feelings. Another person has entered our life: a convincing and inspiring figure whom we can follow; a figure perhaps amiable—but also the embodiment of a truth already familiar to us which had hitherto seemed incomprehensible, hard, and cold.

In such a meeting each of us can share in the Christian event. Such participation happens when Christ or the Christian truth becomes visible to us. According to Giussani, the encounter bears in itself the meaning for which the heart yearns. It becomes for us the source of tenderness toward ourselves and love for others, the medium we live in, the grounding of life and death. Each of us—not just called to a particular vocation—has this opportunity. Each Christian can experience in this encounter baptism's particular significance in his life, the deep communion with the Lord who died and rose from the dead, the grace and the imperatives that spring from such communion. Faith can be born or grow, when a witness crosses one's path. The human encounter, the spirit-filled presence of the other, becomes the bridge that leads us to Christ.

A business consultant was once invited to a large ecclesial assembly. At the very start he said: "People don't interest us. Our goal is efficient administration." None of the priests present appeared to be shocked. What would become of the Church's mission if the view of technocrats were to prevail in her?

MINISTERIAL AUTHORITY AS PRIVILEGE OF RANK

Political and social systems, if treated as absolutes, disfigure the ministry. That both modes of thought are gradually gaining ground, even in the Church, is a reflection of our modern conception of life and the influences exerted on us by daily experience.

However, it is not current trends and the evolution of modern thought alone that have a negative effect on our understanding of ministry. For the misunderstanding of ministry and of its foundation also correspond to a decidedly traditional mentality. That is the case with a juridical reduction of ministry.

In the view of many people, ordained ministers should be socially set apart from the other members of the Church. Their image should be clearly distinguished; it should not be socially blurred. To achieve this goal, it is said, ordained ministers should primarily be seen as members of a particular state or class. Typical of this view is the formulation in a preconciliar manual of canon law: "Through the Sacrament of Ordination ordinands are invested, in an ontological and lasting manner, with sacred powers for the sacramental action of the Church, and in particular for the celebration of the Holy Eucharist. The selection thus made from the members of the Church is based on what, according to the constitution of the Church, is the essential difference between clerics and laity, between those who lead and those who are led."[12]

This and similar statements have contributed to the spreading of a mentality that no longer takes into account all the distinctions made by the canonical prescriptions and their interpretation, but concentrates solely on the view that to become an ordained minister primarily means a special privilege and a special status. Membership in this privileged state is distinguished by precisely defined obligations and especially by powers clearly distinguished from those of the laity. The details of the ordained state arouse interest—less so the theological foundations by which they are justified. The canonical definition of ministry is regarded as sufficient unto itself instead of being drawn from truths of revelation and the doctrine of the Church that transcend it. Upheavals result only when the canonical prescriptions are altered, e.g., when a woman religious speaks from the pulpit.

---

[12] E. Eichmann, K. Mörsdorf, *Lehrbuch des Kirchenrechts*, vol. 2. Paderborn, 1950, 96f.

For canon law had taken the conception of ministry described here as fixed and immutable.

In this way members of the Church have tried to rescue or retrieve something of so-called "premodern society" and revive it in our time. According to sociology, the Church was distinguished by the fact that it had a ruling class; members of this class were invested with political and legislative powers, as well as with military and religious leadership. A special prerogative to rule was accorded to it. In virtue of it, ordained ministers had acquired special qualities through admission to a higher state and belonging to a "leadership elite." Various privileges had been given to them; they were inseparably bound up with their state. Their dignity was determined by their rank.

The main defect of this "juridical" conception of ministry is lack of faith, lack of recognition of the divine grace that is the source of ministry in the Church: it ignores the spiritual character of the ordained minister as Christ's gift. It misunderstands the priest's character as a kind of personal property. It identifies the empowerment given the priest by ordination with the person of the priest, in much the same way that a title of nobility given to a man remains with him indefinitely, even if the king who granted it dies or is deposed. In this way, however, the presence of Christ in the ordained minister is obscured. The servant, who originally was supposed to make present the redemptive mission of Christ, comes to appear as himself the bringer of salvation.

This juridical reduction of ministry is no theoretical construct. It is already encountered in the time of the early Church: and is represented by the heresy of Donatism, which based its teachings on Saint Cyprian of Carthage († 258). According to Cyprian, a sacrament is only administered well when the person who administers it is imbued with the Holy Spirit and lives in the unity of the Church. But when he lives in sin, not only is the effect of the sacrament null and void, but the sin of the priest is transferred, almost like an infection, to the person who receives it.

Cyprian's interpretation acquired far-reaching significance, especially when the emperor Diocletian promulgated his edict against the Christians in February 303. He demanded *inter alia* the destruction of churches and the expropriation of all copies of Holy Scripture in the possession of Christians. Anyone who submitted to the emperor's order was considered a traitor among Christians; a *traditor*. If the traitor happened to be a bishop or other cleric, he was, according to the then widely accepted African theology of Cyprian, no longer able to administer the sacraments in a fruitful and valid way.

What conception of the Church lies behind such a theology? The life of the great bishop of Carthage provides some clues. Cyprian had hardly received the education typical of the jurists and legislators of his time, yet he belonged to the rank of senators, had acquired insights into the workings of state administration and the positive potential of the rule of law. This knowledge of the workings of late-Roman government impacted on his conception of the position of the bishop in the community. He understood it according to the model of senior Roman administrators in the state apparatus. The idea of the bishop's ministerial authority was especially developed according to this model. His interpretation of heresy, for example, is defined by such secular terms as "conspiracy" and "sedition," as if heresy were to be suppressed by the application of penal law and judgment by the courts. In this way Cyprian fostered a juridical concept of the Church through his action and through his writings. He powerfully underlined and absolutized the Church's objective social role.

For Cyprian, therefore, the profound spiritual dimension of the Church and her members merged with their conduct, which could be evaluated, judged, and, if necessary, punished from outside. The Church, in his view, was equivalent to the visible structure of the Church that could be grasped in its objective phenomena. The metaphysical nature of the Church, the transparency of her relationship with God, was in a certain sense obscured. The ordained ministry's link to God was no longer fully perceived. This "juridical" conception of the Church was to emerge even more strongly in those who would draw on Cyprian's theology decades later.

Saint Augustine opposed the Donatist error with a profound investigation of the quality of the ordained minister.[13] He asked whether the ordained minister could claim for himself a special authority (*potestas*) for his apostolic activity. By *potestas* he understood a power invested in the priest by virtue of his own inner capacity, not one conferred on him by an external mandate— one could say: a power he possesses without entering into any relationship. Augustine replied to the Donatist heresy as follows: Servants "are only adopted sons: only to the first-born is *potestas* given." So *potestas* remains the exclusive prerogative of Christ: it is not transferred by the Lord to any man. It follows that the ordained minister has the quality of a servant. Servanthood is the part assigned to the person administering the sacrament in the economy of salvation. That is why Augustine also rejected the Donatist description of the priest as mediator; for if a role of mediation were to be assigned to the priest, the ordained minister would, in Augustine's view, acquire an unjustified independence that could obstruct union with Christ as source of salvation. Augustine refuses to act as the Donatists did; he refers in particular to "Parmenianus [who] in one of his sermons places the bishop as mediator between God and his people."[14]

In his opposition to the theology of the Donatists, Augustine achieves an important confirmation of the mainspring and effectiveness of ministerial action: Christ himself is at work when the sign of the sacrament is placed and the word that interprets it is spoken; he remains the only source and ground of hope in the salvific process. So any fearful question about the worthiness or state of grace of the minister can be put aside; doubts about the effectiveness of the sacramental sign are unnecessary.

---

[13] Cf. especially *In Johannes Evangelium Tractatus*, 5–7; PL 35, 1417 ff.

[14] See Augustine's anti-Donatist sermon, above 33–36.

"If the Lord Jesus Christ had wished to transfer to any one of his servants authority to administer baptism in his stead, he could have done so by divesting himself of the power to baptize and transferring it to any of his servants. To the baptism administered by that servant he could have conferred the same effectiveness as the baptism administered by himself. But he chose not to do so, so that the hope of those who have been baptized should rest in him who had baptized them. He did not wish therefore that the servant should place his hope in other servants."[15]

Saint Augustine's affirmations help to demarcate and define the limitations of empirical categories for the theology of ministry. So long as these categories can be integrated in the horizon of faith and are not in opposition to the explicit relationship to God of the Church's service, the structure of service in the Church can be interpreted by drawing on non-theological concepts. It goes without saying, however, that any steps in this direction should only be taken with extreme caution. The cornerstone that holds together the institution of ministry must clearly and unequivally be the origin of ministerial service in the triune God—and this origin cannot be tacitly presupposed: it needs to be articulated in words.

Common modes of thinking and speaking, as they are proposed to us by the world and society, cannot be applied to theology without prior critical scrutiny. Here it is clear that not all the concepts and behavioral models in circulation today can be helpfully applied to the priest to help him understand his service and identity. Pope Benedict has warned against any kind of "ecclesiological relativism." Signs of such relativism in the Church of our time need to watched with extreme caution and their dissemination checked.

---

[15] Augustine, op.cit (note 13) 5,7; PL 35,1417.

᎒ 11

PASTORAL ASSISTANTS
AND DEACONS
ARGUMENTS IN SUPPORT
OF THE SACRAMENT OF ORDINATION

This service, in which we are entirely given over to others, this giving of what does not come from us, is what in the language of the Church is called sacrament [. . .].

Here a person does not exploit his own powers and capacities: here a person is not installed as a functionary, because he can do something particularly well, or because he has a taste for something or simply because he can earn his daily bread by holding this job. Here what's at issue is not a job in which a man can use his skills to ensure his livelihood, and then perhaps improve his position by rising up the career ladder.

Sacrament means: I give what I cannot give myself; I do what I cannot do myself; I have been sent on a mission and have become the messenger of what the other has transmitted to me. That's why no one can of his own accord declare himself to be a priest. That's why no community can, by its own decisions empower anyone to be a priest. Only from the sacrament can a person receive what belongs to God, and enter into the mission that turns him into God's messenger and tool. And so it follows that only this self-giving to others, this dispossession of self, and the selflessness of this service, can become the source of human maturation and self-fulfilment. For in this self-oblation we are configured to the trinitarian mystery; in other words, our having been created in the image and likeness of God is fulfilled in us and the fundamental model by which we were created is realized. Since we were created in the trinitarian image, it remains true for each of us, at the deepest level, that only he who loses his life will find it [Mt 10:39].

—*Benedict XVI—Joseph Ratzinger, Zur Gemeinschaft gerufen—Kirche heute verstehen,* Freiburg: Herder Verlag, 1991/2005, pp.111–112

ENGAGEMENT IN THE CHURCH

Postconciliar discussion and developments within the Church have not only altered the image of the ordained minister, but have also led to the emergence of new groups of committed lay Catholics and their assumption of pastoral tasks in local communities. One need only think of the numerous voluntary assistants who help ordained ministers in their pastoral tasks: those who participate in parish councils, in Caritas groups or in mission projects; or those who assist in the distribution of communion or as lectors in divine service. The number of full-time professional staff employed in the Church's pastoral services has also increased. If in the past so-called lay theologians were engaged almost exclusively in religious education in schools, now academically trained pastoral staff are supplanting pastoral volunteers in community service. In Germany, a total of 3,018 professional lay staff, both men and women, were employed by the Church in 2006; according to the data of the German bishops' conference, "their number has constantly risen and almost doubled since 1990 (plus 95.7%)."[1] In Austria a total of 957 such staff were registered in 2006. In Switzerland an overall number of 563 lay pastoral assistants were registered in 2005; that is equivalent to a growth of 299% since 1983.

---

[1] German Bishops' Conference, *Arbeitshilfen* no. 221, Bonn, 2008, 33.

POSTCONCILIAR REORGANIZATION OF PASTORAL CARE

The roots of this proliferation of new professional roles in the Church can be traced back to the synods and church assemblies held in various countries in the postconciliar period. In Germany the catalyst was the Würzburg Synod (1972–75). In their spring plenary assembly in 1977, the German bishops debated for almost two days before reaching a consensus that would enable them to convert the impulses coming from the synod into a final document. They further developed in this way the reflections that had already been focal points of discussion at the bishops' plenary assembly in Fulda in 1975. Twenty years after the Würzburg Synod, they finally issued the declaration *Der pastorale Dienst in der Pfarrgemeinde* (Pastoral service in the parish community).[2]

In this document the bishops reviewed the new spheres of services in the Church, with the aim of attributing a well-defined form to them. These spheres comprised both the missionary task of all members of the Church, as founded in the common priesthood of the faithful, and the particular responsibility of the ministry, which had long been exclusively reserved for bishops and priests. The German bishops' conclusions about pastoral service in parishes rested on the documents of the Second Vatican Council, on those of the mentioned above synod, and on other texts relating to the ministry of the Church; they paid special attention to the role of lay assistants who participate more closely in the specific tasks of the ministry.

In all postconciliar directives regarding the structure of service in the Church, the diaconate—theologically considered—occupies a special position. Vatican II had after intensive discussions opted for the permanent diaconate of married men. The declaration of the German bishops in 1995 also attributed a particular quality to

---

[2] Issued by the secretariat of the German Bishops' Conference, Bonn, 1995.

this diaconate, since "by virtue of the Sacrament of Ordination it participates in the three fundamental services of the ministry" (2.4).

The regulatory system established by the German bishops for lay participation in pastoral services touches on many other aspects; further details can be found in the published document. Though many problems relating to the more general problem of pastoral care remained unanswered—the then-president of the German Bishops' Conference, Bishop, now Cardinal, Lehmann, spoke of a "consensus document" and an "interim review"— our attention here will be limited to the systematic theological implications of pastoral service in the parish community; or more precisely to this question: Have the pastors of the Church so far sufficiently taught pastoral consultants and pastoral assistants about the significance and grace of the Sacrament of Ordination to the diaconate? More particularly: Have they done so in ways that conform to the existing sacramental order of the Church, which reserves this sacrament exclusively for male candidates? Even to pose this question sometimes seems like breaking a taboo. When the German bishops attached particular emphasis to the diaconate in their pastoral instruction of 1975, criticisms were not slow in coming: Did the bishops perhaps have the intention of imposing a "solution from above . . . wholly at variance with practice?" Did they act from "embarrassment, or even from fear" in not assigning any solid basis to the commitment of pastoral assistants?[3] A 400-page information-packed dossier with the title *Der Beruf des Pastoralreferenten*[4] on the role of (lay) pastoral consultants in the Church did not even pose the question.

Such hysterical fears in reference to the Sacrament of Ordination undoubtedly rest on misunderstandings. The diaconate is not aimed at attaining ecclesiastical power or defending vested interests. Its meaning for the Church is theological in nature: it corresponds to a particular responsibility for the building up

---

[3] Cf. the fears expressed in the *Public Forum* of May 21, 1976, 18 f.

[4] Georg Köhl, *Der Beruf des Pastoralreferenten*. Freiburg/Schweiz, 1987.

of the community. The gifts necessary to succeed in this undertaking are conferred by grace through the Sacrament of Ordination. Through ordination the deacon is irrevocably placed by Christ at the service of the Church; he is spiritually prepared and sent out on his mission through the power of the Spirit and the mandate of the Church. This faith in the sacrament of the diaconate has clearly made little impression on the consciousness of the Church. It needs to be proclaimed anew—not least, in view of the interest aroused by the profession of pastoral assistants. Otherwise there could be a lingering suspicion that the emphasis given to the sacrament of the diaconate was prompted by an overcautious ecclesiastical policy and that the legitimate expectations of lay theologians were simply being ignored.

VATICAN II AND PASTORAL SERVICES

The Second Vatican Council recognized the laity's ability to perform pastoral services in the Church. For the laity participate in the threefold ministry of Christ. From the apostolate of the laity and their sharing in the mission of the Church, it follows that they also have "the capacity of being appointed by the hierarchy to some ecclesiastical offices with a view to a spiritual end" (*Lumen Gentium* no. 33). This capacity is expressed in other conciliar documents. However, the fact that this qualification is limited to some specific situations should not be overlooked.[5]

Studies in canon law have therefore in no way concluded from these statements on the involvement of the laity in the apostolate that the Council meant to extend blanket authorization for the extension of ministerial functions to the laity. They point out in the first place that the laity's field of pastoral activity is the personal apostolate, not public ministerial activity, which primarily rests on the ability to transmit sacramental gifts which have been received.[6] The conferral of the office of proclaiming

---

[5] Cf. *LG* 35; and the Decree on the Apostolate of Lay People (*Apostolicam Actuositatem*), no. 17.
[6] Alvaro del Portillo, *Gläubige und Laien in der Kirche*. Paderborn, 1972, 170 f.

the Word of God in public not in private, is not in the strict sense a right; it is bound up with the official mandate of the Church, the so-called *missio canonica*. The Council further granted to the laity in exceptional circumstances the faculty to fill in for priests: "when there are no sacred ministers, or when these are impeded under persecution, some lay people supply sacred functions to the best of their ability" (*LG* 35). The activity envisaged is grounded on an authorization to substitute for the ordained in exceptional circumstances; it will therefore always have an extraordinary character. It involves, for example, the liturgy of the Word, the extraordinary administration of baptism, and the distribution of Holy Communion.[7]

It would thus be overinterpreting Vatican II to find in its decrees an intention on the Council's part to authorize the laity to assume ministerial functions, other than as an interim measure in exceptional circumstances.[8] These texts seek only to make the point that, in some particular emergency situations, ensuring the continuing provision of pastoral services within the community might require dispensing with the grace of the sacrament in the carrying out of some particular activities.

An important contribution for the discussion of the problems at issue here is made by Vatican II's decree on the Church's Missionary Activity *Ad gentes*. The Decree emphasized the importance of diaconal ordination: "It would help those men who carry out the ministry of a deacon—preaching the word of God as catechists, governing scattered Christian communities in the name of the bishop or parish priest, or exercising charity in the performance of social or charitable works—if they were to be strengthened by the imposition of hands which has come down from the apostles. They would be more closely bound to

---

[7] Ibid., 206; see also Peter Krämer, *Dienst und Vollmacht in der Kirche*. Trier, 1973, 62ff.; and Ulrich Mosiek, *Verfassungsrecht der lateinischen Kirche* I. Freiburg, 1975, 191 ff., 217ff.

[8] Exceptions to this rule are lay experts who provide specialized professional expertise to Church institutions; cf. Decree on the Apostolate of Lay People (*Apostolicam Actuositatem*), no. 22: *Laici qui seipsos sua peritia professionali devovent* (Laypeople who dedicate themselves with their own professional expertise).

the altar and their ministry would be made more fruitful through the sacramental grace of the diaconate" (no. 16).

Just this passage is cited by the *Motu Proprio* of Pope Paul VI *Sacrum Diaconatus* of June 18, 1967, which directly refers to the regulation of the pastoral services performed by deacons. In its introduction we find the following clarification: "Even if some tasks of the diaconate are in fact entrusted to the laity, especially in mission territories, nonetheless it is appropriate that men who do in fact exercise a diaconal service [...] be strengthened by the imposition of hands as transmitted by the apostles and be more closely bound to the altar, so that they may be able more effectively to perform their service with the help of the sacramental grace of the diaconate."

THE BEST POSSIBLE REQUISITES

As this quotation suggests, determining the role of pastoral assistants and deacons within the Church and defining their spheres of action will depend largely on how the question of their service is posed. What is it that characterizes their role? That these lay assistants are effective members of the Church by virtue of their baptism alone may seem a sufficient response to those who attempt to define their role in terms of what constitutes the indispensable minimum of sacramental roots and qualification by divine grace. In that case, at the level of objective grace, these servants of the Church cannot be distinguished from those who take no responsibility for service in the Church. Their activity would therefore seem to be founded on a purely canonical mandate. If, however, we seek the best possible criteria to mark out the spiritual qualifications for the service they render, we must conclude that it is the plenitude of the grace offered by Revelation that inspires and perpetuates forms of ecclesial service: in short, the grace that is given by the Sacrament of Ordination. Moreover, this striving to find the best possible criteria will also make the Church's reliance on God's help clearer both to lay assistants and communities. It will bring home to them that it is by way of sacramental guarantee that the Church can best perform her mission. At this point, candidates for service in the Church must ask themselves how such services can be performed without the added grace of the sacrament. That is why they need, as a matter of urgency, to be informed of the reasons why they should ask the Church for permission to receive the Sacrament of Ordination to the diaconate. In short, rather than dwelling on the indispensable minimum required for those who wish to perform services in the Church, we should choose the perspective of their best possible spiritual qualification.

I shall now try to sum up in the form of three theses the theological foundations for the diaconate as the first step of the Sacrament of Holy Orders, as formulated by Vatican II and as offered, after sometimes bitter controversies, also to married men:

I. The New Testament, the conciliar texts on the renewal of the diaconate, and the liturgy of ordination interpret the special sacramental quality attached to diaconal ordination as an empowerment by the Holy Spirit distinct from the grace already conferred by baptism and confirmation. On the other hand, this sacramental quality can only be regarded as the prerequisite for ecclesial service if it is not understood as tied to any specific or clearly delimited field, but as qualifying candidates for pastoral service in general and ensuring that those who perform such services do so as ordained ministers. The services that deacons can perform are specified by Paul VI's *Motu Proprio*, in addition to what is said in the Constitution on the Church *Lumen Gentium* (cf. *LG* 29): they include liturgical assistance to the bishop and priest; solemn celebration of baptism; assistance in the celebration of the rite of matrimony; funeral rites and preaching during the celebration of the Eucharist (*Sacrum Diaconatus* no. 22). These specific "diaconal services" must continue to be reserved for the deacon, so that no new "ministry without ordination," such as "lay deacons" or "preachers," arise or develop in the

Church. In all cases it should be taken for granted that the mission to which deacons are called is permanent; for the office of the diaconate is by its sacramental nature permanent and cannot therefore be considered a qualification for a commitment of limited duration or a temporary mandate.

2. Qualification for the deaconate is guaranteed by the prayer of the Church and the imposition of the bishop's hands. Ordination provides not only the sacramental foundations of the canonical authorization to perform particular activities, but also the authority to act in the role of deputy *hierarchiae nomine* in various fields (*Sacrum Diaconatus* no. 22.9). By diaconal ordination the deacon is firmly incorporated in the circle of those who hold ministerial responsibilities in the Church (ibid. no. 23).

3. The formulary of ordination makes it clear that ordination creates a personal closeness of the ordinand to Christ. This close personal bond with Christ has particular consequences for the deacon's spiritual activities. In his life the deacon must make room for the sacramentally transmitted reality of Christ to be expressed in all that he does.

KARL RAHNER'S REFLECTIONS

The fundamental presuppositions regarding the diaconate, as deduced from the texts of Vatican II and the postconciliar statements of the Apostolic See, can also be explored by considering the pronouncements of dogmatic theologians. A *ratio theologica* accompanies and underpins the Church's authoritative teachings on the diaconate. Here it will be presented with particular reference to a pioneering theological study by Karl Rahner: *Die Theologie der Erneuerung des Diakonates* (The theology of the renewal of the diaconate). The author had already laid out these views in 1962. This gives the lie to any suspicion of partisanship.[9]

---

[9]The page numbers interpolated in the text refer to *Diaconia in Christo*, edited by Karl Rahner and Herbert Vorgrimler, Freiburg, 1962.

In determining the spiritual foundations for ecclesial activities no one can deny that God can grant his grace also independently of the Sacrament of Ordination; it follows that, in relation to grace, someone engaged in ecclesial service can never be dependent in an *absolute* way on the Sacrament of Ordination. Despite that, Rahner argues as follows: "Where the conferral of a ministry and the divine guarantee of the necessary grace for the fulfillment of the ministry can be provided in a sacramental way (and be performed in a meaningful and practical way), it should so be provided" (301). In other comparable cases, that is how the Church acts. Theologians therefore begin from the presupposition that the reception of some sacraments is not under all circumstances obligatory; the reception of confirmation, the anointing of the sick, confession or the frequent reception of the Eucharist are not subject to any absolute divine obligation. In spite of that, in conformity with the practice and the doctrine of the Church, it seems incumbent on the Church to encourage the faithful to receive these sacraments.

Behind this viewpoint lies a deeper motivation: namely, the Church's amply confirmed conviction that God's love for man should be expressed as far as possible, in sacramental form, for the sake of both the individual and the Church. This interpretation agrees with the fundamental structure of God's work of salvation; for its structure and the order of salvation bound up with it is the order of the Word of God that became flesh. The unity between the pouring out of the Spirit in the faith and the ecclesiological incarnation of the Spirit is determined in it once and for all; the objective presence of the Church and the presence of the Spirit by which she is animated can no longer be separated in the eschatological situation of the Church. As Karl Rahner puts it: "Where sacramental grace can be conferred in the framework of what is humanly possible and meaningful, it should be conferred; indeed it is fundamentally to be recommended and is opportune, and this opportuneness should not be dismissed with the objection that, in the last analysis, the grace could be obtained without the sacrament" (302).

The impact this rationale has upon the faith and devotion of those to be ordained also reinforces the need to affirm qualification for ministerial service by ordination. It is likely that anyone called to the ministry in a sacramental way will, by virtue of the uniqueness of the event and the permanent effect of the sacramental grace, respond in a far more radical manner than if qualification for service occured in some other way. In addition, the sacramental qualification for service will have positive effects on the community itself. The appeal, dissemination, and appreciation of this service among the faithful will be decidedly improved.

Parenthetically, it should be said that the thorny question of whether female pastoral assistants should also be qualified for service in the Church by ordination to the diaconate will not be considered here. In the present context we limit ourselves to reflecting on the relation between the pastoral service and a sacrament *offered* by the Church. At present the Sacrament of Holy Orders is offered only to men, not to women.

The consultations and decisions of the Second Vatican Council reinstituted in the Church the diaconal stage of the Sacrament of Ordination as an autonomous ministry of service. Today it is still worth considering what was originally intended by the revival of this stage of ordination. Karl Rahner's remarks on the Church's doctrine of grace and sacrament[10] are of such a fundamental nature that any order of services in the Church that ignores them cannot be described as successful.

ARGUMENTS FROM THE SOCIOLOGY OF KNOWLEDGE AND THE SOCIOLOGY OF ORGANIZATIONS

The guidelines of sacramental theology are also of considerable importance for deacons. In examining the structure of pastoral

---

[10] That Karl Rahner continued to hold fast to this interpretation even after the introduction of the diaconate can be inferred from his paper: 'Ansatzpunkte für eine Spiritualität des Priesters vom Amt her gesehen,' in: *Priesterliche Spiritualität heute*, edited by Stefan Laszlo. Wien, 1977, here 115 ff.

services in the Church and considering the appropriate theological place for preparing lay theologians for this service, we can find further corroborating evidence if we leave to one side for the moment the perspective of theology and consider the matter from a sociological point of view. Arguments can be derived from both the sociology of knowledge and the sociology of organizations. They help to underline the systematic theological reflection briefly recalled above. So it is useful to bring them into our argument, if only briefly.[11]

The process of the institutionalization of social phenomena has often been described. An institution is an organization with an objective presence, even independently of human participation in it. Thus the institution of fatherhood, for example, does not exist only after a man's first child recognizes its existence. It is considered to exist even independently of the persons it incorporates and the relationship to it thus established. So institutions are seen to transcend the individual and necessarily claim authority over the individual; and the conduct of the individual in the preestablished institutional framework in which he/she is incorporated represents an important help both for the individual and for society: the transmission to the next generation of the models of conduct enshrined in the institution fulfills an important social role while relieving the individual of a burden. The institution, in other words, frees the individual from having constantly to make new decisions for himself. It is through institutions that, in the human consciousness, the world gains in stability and thus acquires the essential preconditions for invention and innovation. Institutions are perpetuated in society because they are recognized as the "'permanent' solution of a 'permanent' problem" (Berger, 74).

However, the preservation and transmission of the knowledge of which the institution is custodian cannot simply be taken

---

[11] The following remarks rest on two sociological publications: Peter Berger and Thomas Luckmann, *Die gesellschaftliche Konstruktion der Wirklichkeit. Eine Theorie der Wissenssoziologie*. Frankfurt, 1974; and Niklas Luhmann, *Funktionen und Folgen formaler Organisation*. Berlin, 1972.

for granted. Let us take hunting as an example: The various techniques of hunting, the proper weapons to use, the species of animals to be hunted, rules about how they ought to be shot, the establishment of seasons, etc.—all this represents a kind of storehouse of knowledge that transmits behavioral prescriptions that are an inseparable part of the institution in question. Access to this knowledge must be possible whenever the existence of a society needs to be defended, for instance, a society at the hunter-gatherer cultural stage.

This preservation and transmission of knowledge is conceivable in the first instance through teaching. In the case of an objective storehouse of knowledge common to a majority of a society's active members, it is also possible through *representation*. Those who perform such representation will personify, and at the same time represent, an institution's objective meaning: they will act as its role bearers. Through such roles institutions penetrate the individual experience and are indispensable means of transmitting institutionalized forms of conduct. Thus, for example, the role of the judge represents the institution of the rule of law as a whole. This institution is represented, and its social experience transmitted, through roles. "With its ensemble of programmed actions this role is rather like the unwritten text of a stageplay, whose performance depends on the recurrent representation of prescribed roles by living actors. The actors personify their roles and recreate the drama anew by performing it on the stage. Neither a stage play nor an institution could exist without such a realization that is repeated ever anew. Thus if we maintain that roles represent institutions, we are also led to infer that roles permit institutions to exist and to be experienced anew, and made present anew, by living human beings" (Berger, 79). So the institution needs to be represented through roles; the institution needs to be given new life by the vital human conduct of those who perform the roles on which its existence depends.

When need arises, roles for the representation of a particular institutional reality in society need to be given particular emphasis, since not every part in the 'performance,' not every 'actor,' is equally important for the maintenance of the institution. Such emphasizing of roles seems all the more necessary if the norms and values represented by the institution are perceived as problematic by society as a whole. In particular, a rapidly changing social environment will represent a major obstacle to the maintenance of fixed behavioral schemes and situational models. In these cases, leadership roles are especially needed, as the sociology of organizations underlines. In their social context they are presumed to embody the principles of justice. That is why the stabilization of endangered institutions can be expected of them more than of others. However, they are obliged as much as possible to identity themselves with the role they play.

As an alternative to the process of change in a social context, leadership roles accentuate the element of continuity; the unambiguity of their mode of conduct (endorsed by the tradition they represent) is a corrective to ambivalent models of conduct. "The members of the institution who assume leadership roles must consciously and lastingly conduct themselves as leaders. They obey a particular discipline since their conduct is under the observation of other members and of the outside world" (Luhmann, 208).

Every society has institutions of a transcendent sort. Even societies that declare themselves to be atheistic develop pseudo-religious practices. The purpose of the Church as an institution is to transmit to society and to believers the fullness of the revelation that powerfully entered the world in the person of Christ. The Church is placed at the service of the maintenance and transmission of the truth of the faith and its practice. Insofar as she is an institution, the laws identified by sociology as governing institutions in general hold good for her. Ministry in the Church in its institutional aspect is also covered by these insights. It follows that the leadership roles of ordained ministers are all the more necessary in times of rapid change.

That the distinctive features of the ordained ministry defined by the Church correspond in many respects to the leadership role described in the theory of institutions can be expressed as follows:

1. Ordained ministers are the living actors who perform the roles prescribed for them and thus represent the meaning of the Church as an institution. They perform their roles in daily life in myriad different situations; they do so in a unique way in the celebration of the liturgy. Only by their continuing performance does the Church as an institution continue to exist and to be experienced ever anew by men and women in our time.

2. The role conferred on the ordained minister is permanent and integrates him firmly into the ecclesial system: for ordination implies an irrevocable relationship with Christ and his Church.

3. Those who assume the role assigned to them are bound to identify themselves with it as an essential element of the system they represent. This is also the case in ordination, since identification with the role of ordained minister is not a matter of socially prescribed typecasting of personal response to grace received and to the mission one is called to perform. The ordained minister identifies himself with his role by creating space for the sacramentally transmitted reality of Christ in all his activity.

That is why sociological findings appear to corroborate the theological conclusion that people interested in service in the Church should be persuaded if possible to pursue the goal of ordination. That also holds true for the case in which—as in some individual activities performed by a deacon—ordination is not obligatory.

The arguments presented here regarding ordained ministry, and more particularly the diaconate, are not aimed at achieving a stabilization of the Church as an institution, but at making the aim of this institution easier to bear. Sociologically considered, the objective of an institution is always that of transmitting a body of knowledge and relieving the burden of individuals in relation to what it represents. With regard to the Catholic Church, the aim of the Church as an institution is the teaching of models of conduct consolidated in the faith, both at the liturgical and at the private, ethical levels ("that's what we do"). It relieves believers of the burden of having to bear their responsibilities alone. It also provides for a cognitive and emotional reinterpretation of central truths of the faith by "experts," in other words credible witnesses. The main function of the institution is precisely to reduce uncertainty to a minimum. This is precisely in line with the qualities of leadership roles as described above.

ஃ 12

GOD AS MYSTAGOGUE
INDIVIDUAL RELIGIOUS SENSE
AND ECCLESIAL WAY OF SALVATION

In the Christian tradition "conscience," "*con-scientia*," means "with knowledge": that is, ourselves, our being is open and can listen to the voice of being itself, the voice of God. Thus, the voice of the great values is engraved in our being and the greatness of the human being is precisely that he is not closed in on himself, he is not reduced to the material, something quantifiable, but possesses an inner openness to the essentials and has the possibility of listening. In the depths of our being, not only can we listen to the needs of the moment, to material needs, but we can also hear the voice of the Creator himself and thus discern what is good and what is bad. Of course, this capacity for listening must be taught and encouraged. The commitment to the preaching that we do in church consists of precisely this: developing this very lofty capacity with which God has endowed human beings for listening to the voice of truth and also the voice of values. I would say, therefore, that the first step would be to make people aware that our very nature carries in itself a moral message, a divine message that must be deciphered. We can become increasingly better acquainted with it and listen to it if our inner hearing is opened and developed.

—*Pope Benedict XVI, Meeting with the Clergy of the dioceses of Belluno-Feltre and Treviso, Church of Saint Justin Martyr, Auronzo di Cadore, July 24, 2007*

Henri de Lubac's study *Catholicisme* came, at the very least, as a surprise when it was first published in France in 1937.[1] It pointed with many proofs to something that hitherto had been rather obscured in the ecclesiology of the time: "The fundamental characteristic of Catholicism is its community dimension; it releases a movement that fosters not only inner spiritual life, but also external communion."[2]

If the book were to appear today, it would seem but the confirmation of a contemporary trend. The reception of community thinking in theology and in pastoral ministry that has taken place in the meantime is in fact impressive. In the final document of the Extraordinary Bishops' Synod in 1985, *Ecclesia sub Verbo* of December 20, 1985, the theologoumenon *communio* occupies a key position. With its help, the theology of the Church was further developed; the bond between unity and diversity elucidated; the relation of the local churches to each other determined; and the participation of the laity in the Church's mission reaffirmed. Without question, few criteria of the Church are now so universally accepted and undisputed as the truth that the Church is communion. On the other hand, it is plausible that this conviction spread so rapidly and achieved such a wide dissemination because it coincided with man's profound and universally shared desire to live in unity.[3]

GROWING INDIVIDUALISM

Of course the movement of the times is not all in the same direction. Trends are not absolute; they also arouse opposition; they make people look at the "other side of the coin." Frustration or apathy may erode the need for community. Passivity or resignation

---

[1] Henri de Lubac, *Catholicisme*. Paris, 1937. English translation: *Catholicism: A Study of Dogma in Relation to the Corporate Destiny of Mankind*. London, 1950.

[2] Henri de Lubac, *Mémoire sur l'occasion de mes écrits*. Namur, 1989, 26.

[3] A good exposition of the *communio* theology of Joseph Ratzinger can be found in Karl-Heinz Menke, *Stellvertretung: Schlüsselbegriff christlichen Lebens und theologische Grundkategorie*. Einsiedeln, 1991, 321–339.

may lead to isolation. Isolation, indeed, may even be justified and proclaimed as the higher condition of life. The media also register the spread of a phenomenon that runs counter to the sense of community: "the ego society—each man for himself and against everyone."[4] The modern lifestyle has cut man adrift from all historically determined social forms and destroyed the relationships that supported them. People must do without the forms of security that formerly offered them a tradition that would shape their lives; or perhaps they are happy simply to throw this tradition overboard, together with everything else that appeared to place limits on them. Clearly, a growing and sometimes extreme individualism is gaining ground in the industrialized countries.[5] Are the sense of community and solidarity threatened?

In his anthropological studies Philipp Lersch maintains that the relationship between society and the individual is determined dialectically (in the Hegelian sense).[6] Society and individual constantly need each other; and it would be inappropriate to eliminate the tension between them in favor of one pole or the other: there is a fruitful reciprocity between them. The author calls this reciprocity *Wechselbezogenheit*, a mutual correlation, which is realized in "social interaction" (224). The individual self does not retreat into passivity but is constantly challenged by the surrounding world and its order and values. Only in this interaction is the individual not flattened, or reduced, to a mere reflection of society; only in this tension does his interaction with society not lead to the loss of human autonomy or reduction to a state of "resounding passivity" (Nietzsche).

---

[4] See the cover title of the magazine *Spiegel* no. 22, 1994.

[5] See Gerhard Schmidtchen, *Ethik und Protest*, Opladen, 1992, which speaks of spreading egoism and the selfish message that it is a "good principle" to live according to one's own needs, to push through one's own agenda, even if that means being hard of heart, and to achieve one's own ideal, even if others don't understand it. This egoism can interestingly be correlated with lapsed faith and absence from Mass; it is very seldom found among regular churchgoers (7%).

[6] Philipp Lersch, *Der Mensch als soziales Wesen*. München, 1965; the page numbers interpolated in the text refer to this book.

That is why the anthropologist warns against the threat of what he calls *sociologism*. He maintains that the industrial revolution of past centuries destructured all our forms of life. In this way the individualism that reigned until the eighteenth century was replaced by collectivism, which sees "the really important goals and values of human life" in society alone (228). This collectivized approach conceals the human face and is interested not in man as an individual but only in society. Mass media, mass culture, mass systems of demand and supply, and the control of the masses have increasingly turned the individual "into a dense network of interpersonal and transpersonal relations and dependencies and reduced his existence to no more than a 'point of intersection'" (Arnold Gehlen) (229).

Not surprisingly contemporary man opposes this impoverishment. Yet people lack the strength to overcome it. For we are living at the present time "in a period dominated by large organizations in which the individual is simply considered as the performer of a function, someone whose social utility can be rationally calculated, a mere cog in a machine who can be replaced at will and whose individuality is of no interest; a period in which the technical means of mass communication can shape opinions and standardize people's wishes" (234).

It hardly needs saying that today, even less than before, is anyone in a position to abandon the ship in which he is crammed together with others. Besides, it is doubtless safer and more comfortable—less of a bother—to do just as others do in choosing lifestyles and behavioral models; to have the same opinions, to think and to speak just like them. The modern age led to conformism, and the postmodern provides even less protection against it. The phenomenon of standardization, the reduction of man to a unit in a standardized mass, is increasingly curbing self-determination. It imposes social conformity and leads to social homogenization. The capacity of the individual to decide for himself is reduced. Each passing ideology and fashion exerts its influence and determines people's lifestyles. Instead of realistic perception and individual initiative, a kind of supine conformism, what Arnold Gehlen calls "acquiescent tractability," is spreading.

The preaching of the Gospel and catechesis cannot help but be rooted in the spiritual movements of society; for their aim is to show modern man how to recognize God's presence in our midst and to teach him God's answers to the questions of our time. The Church, moreover, has openly admitted "how much she has profited from the history and development of mankind" (*Gaudium et Spes* no. 44). So it is natural that her mission of salvation should seek the individual, all the more so in our time. The high estimation of *communio* in theology and pastoral work must never neglect the individual. The sensibility of the Church's pastoral ministry must therefore take seriously the social definition of the individual.[7]

THE GREATNESS OF THE INDIVIDUAL

As a spiritual person, man is more than the representative of a generalized phenomenon: a man is unique. He is not just the embodiment of a general idea. He is the subject of an eternal determination and a definitive destiny. For he is the beneficiary of the direct self-communication of God's benevolence in Jesus Christ. When God loves, he creates what is new. His love must to the highest degree be understood as quite personal and individual. "For the more personal love is—the more it permits the individual person to practice self-giving in love—all the more individual, unique, and irreplaceable does love become" (99).

So God's love is always more than general benevolence, such as is shown by the Creator for his creation or a sovereign for his subjects: an equally distributed, carefully measured out and universally encouraging benevolence. God's love, on the contrary, is particular: God cherishes each individual with a wholly unique

---

[7] On the following see further Karl Rahner, 'Über die heilsgeschichtliche Bedeutung des einzelnen in der Kirche,' in *Sendung und Gnade. Beiträge zur Pastoraltheologie.* Innsbruck, 1959, 89–128.

and incomparable love. That is why the Word of God can also express this love with the imagery of bride and bridegroom; for it is between spouses that love, in human experience, is expressed in its most individual and least vicarious or interchangeable way. This love of the bridegroom for his bride embraces the Chosen People and each individual person chosen by God: "When I passed by you again and looked upon you, behold, you were at the age for love; and I spread my skin over you and covered your nakedness; yea, I plighted my troth to you and entered into a covenant with you, says the Lord God, and you became mine" (Ez 16:8). The partner whom God loves so dearly is unique by virtue of his creative love: "If anyone hears my voice and opens the door, I will come in to him and eat with him, and he with me" (Rev 3:20).

God's founding love awakens an echo in man, which is transformed by grace into spiritual and personal individuality. Such individuality comes from the very heart of the person. It is therefore necessarily more than the result of observance of the law, training, imitation, or social pressure. All these psychological reactions come quite simply from prepersonal layers of consciousness. Even supposing they could by themselves respond to God's love, they would still lack the crucial element: the answering turning of the heart of the person in an act of that individual freedom and responsibility of which God himself is the author. That is why the Church can never tire of devoting her attention to the individual—not least, because the acts born from the spiritual individuality thus granted by grace represent and consummate the inner heart of the life of the Church.

"TASTE FOR GOD" IN SOME FATHERS OF THE CHURCH

These necessarily general reflections on the individual may seem at first sight no more than abstract theories. Yet their truth has been repeatedly and variously confirmed. That is why we can reach them also by induction: by self-observation and observation of others; by the careful scrutiny of spiritual quest and spiritual determination in the inner man; by grasping the guiding hand of God in the human heart. For God does not draw near to the individual once and for all; this show of affection for the individual continues through time. It has a history: and this history of God's presence in the human heart is enduring, ever-changing, and of the utmost importance.

The early Fathers of the Church—at once theologians and pastors—described this history. They can still be spiritual travelling companions today and lead the individual at the personal level to the "taste for God." Their sermons and meditations arouse the certainty that the triune God continuously invites each individual fully to share the happiness that springs from his trinitarian life. The experience that they put into writing, and that every member of the Church can share, is both instructive and inspiring: it teaches and motivates at the same time.

Thus an early patristic source, Irenaeus of Lyon († *c.*202) teaches that man can observe in himself that which brings him closer to God or removes him further from him; and, by this knowledge of good and evil, man is taught that it is incomparably better to be close to God. Irenaeus develops a kind of theological rule for the individual way of salvation: what goes for the Old Testament People of God also is true for the individual Christian: it is through the experience of deprivation or disobedience that God strengthens man in his experience of God's closeness. The experience of God is present in the personal experience of good and evil:

> Since God, therefore, gave [to man] such greatness of mind (*magnanimitatem*), man knew both the good of obedience and the evil of disobedience, so that the eye of the mind, receiving experience of both, may with judgment make choice of what is better; and that he may never become indolent or neglectful of God's commandment; and learning by experience that it is an evil thing which deprives him of life, that is, disobedience to

God, may never attempt it at all, but knowing that what preserves his life, namely obedience to God, is good, he may diligently keep it with all earnestness. [...] That is why man is given a twofold experience, possessing knowledge of both kinds, so that with discipline he may choose what is better. How indeed, if he had no knowledge of the contrary, could he have been taught what is good? For there is a surer and more undeniable comprehension of matters submitted to us than the mere surmise arising from an opinion about them. For just as the tongue receives experience of sweet and bitter by means of tasting, and the eye discriminates between black and white by means of vision, and the ear recognizes the distinction of sounds by hearing; so also does the mind, by receiving the knowledge of what is good through the experience of both [good and evil], become more tenacious of its preservation, by acting in obedience to God.[8]

The martyr bishop develops his fundamental theological argument on God's individual guidance of man in various contexts. Sometimes he maintains that it presupposes the incarnation of Christ: without the experience of Christ's passion and death, we could never achieve the experience of life in God. "He became the Son of man to habituate man to receive God and to habituate God to receive man."[9]

Origen († 254) added further theological insights concerning the process of man's knowledge of God and developed a spiritual theology on the basis of the biblical experience of God. Finding guidance for his theology not only in the biblical evidence but in Greek thought, he reached the conclusion that man can only possess what he has actually experienced. Origen understood "experience" in this sense in two ways: it is "the result of a long and laborious process of making it one's own through time, and thus experiencing what God (for man) truly is."[10]

---

[8] Irenaeus of Lyon, *Adversus haereses* 4.39.1 (SC 100,2, 954f.).

[9] Ibid., 3.20.2 (SC 211,392).

[10] Hans Urs von Balthasar, *Herrlichkeit I. Schau der Gestalt.* Einsiedeln, 1961, 256.

Later fourth-century homilies of the Egyptian anchorite Saint Macarius Alexandrinus developed in greater detail the process that leads the individual to the mystical encounter with God. Two thoughts of Macarius are of particular relevance for our reflection.

1. The Son of God, who abased himself by becoming man, restored to the splendor of the light the fallen soul that had become obscured and distanced itself from God by sin. This first takes place at the interior and spiritual level, but at the eschatological level is made bodily manifest.

2. Spiritual experience is not necessarily definitive; it is not vouchsafed once and for all. Those who have been illuminated by the Spirit may fall once again and must constantly struggle to preserve the gifts they have received. Prayer and asceticism gradually help us to overcome sin and lead to the victory of good over evil.

The presupposition for the return to God is the Word that became flesh: the incarnation of the *Logos*. It is the positive expression of his love that enables man, through the experience of the senses, to recognize God's spiritual love. The *Logos* becomes tangible; it becomes flesh for holy souls, insofar as they can grasp it. God embodies himself "according to the subtlety of the soul's nature," so that He, who is invisible, be seen, so that He, who is impalpable, be felt:

> [Holy souls] should feel his sweetness, and enjoy in real experience the goodness of the light of that ineffable enjoyment. When he pleases, he becomes fire, which burns up every base passion that has been introduced into the soul; "for our God is a consuming fire" (Heb 12:29). When he pleases, he is rest unspeakable, unutterable, that the soul may rest in the Godhead's own rest. When he pleases, he is joy and peace, which both cherish and protect the soul.[11]

---

[11] Macarius Alexandrinus, *Homily* 4.11 (PTS 4,36,174–179). For an English translation: A.J. Mason, *Fifty Spiritual Homilies of Saint Macarius the Egyptian*. London: Society for Promoting Christian Knowledge, 1921, here 26.

Typical of the individual and personal approach is the way Macarius transforms the great images of the biblical tradition into existential models. Thus, the (apocryphal) image of Christ's descent into hell, that serves to restore humankind to heaven, is applied to the individual: the sinner is in hell and experiences his distance from God as if he were buried alive: "Your own heart is a sepulcher and a tomb"; the river of hell flows in him; he "has been plunged and drowned in the abyss of darkness and the deep of death, and is dead and parted from God." But Christ is the expert swimmer, the diver who is able to "go down into the secret chambers and the depths of hell and death" and bring up out of the darkness "the Adam that lay dead."[12] Of the exodus from Egypt and the journey through the desert Macarius says: "These are mysteries of the soul which are truly brought to pass in a man who earnestly endeavors to come to the promise of life, and is redeemed out of the kingdom of death, and receives the pledge from God, and partakes of the Holy Spirit."[13] Of the resurrection of Lazarus, Macarius says: "Recognize in your innermost being that you bear the same wounds, the same stench, the same darkness. We are all the sons of that dark race. [...] He [the Lord] alone by his coming healed that sore of the soul, that incurable sore."[14]

Lastly, the testimony of Saint Augustine († 430) needs to be heard. His analysis is guided by observations of the reactions of the human soul. The Bishop of Hippo begins with a verse from Saint John's Gospel: "No one can come to me unless the Father who sent me draws him" (6:44). First of all, he underlines that it is the Father who calls and draws the individual, but the individual is not drawn against his will. "What is attracted is the soul, captured by love [...] You are drawn both by free will—but that is too little—and also by desire." What else is at stake when

---

[12] Ibid., 11.10–12 (102, 134ff.); A.J. Mason, op.cit. 85–86.

[13] Ibid., 47.14 (310, 179ff.); A.J. Mason, op. cit. 297.

[14] Ibid., 30.8 (245, 119ff.); A.J. Mason, op. cit. 227.

the psalmist writes: "Take delight in the Lord, and he will give you the desires of your heart" (Ps 37:4)? There is a desire of the heart, says Augustine, to which the bread of heaven tastes sweet. And when Virgil recognizes that each human heart is moved by desire and attracted by what can satisfy it, it is clear that no compulsion, but only desire, is at work; no duty moves, but only joy. "With how much more justice, then, should we say that man is drawn to Christ, when he rejoices in truth, beatitude, justice, and life eternal"?

Augustine then asks himself the following question: If the senses of the body can have their pleasures, why ought not the soul to have them too? But if that were the case, the words of the psalmist would not longer be apt: for, according to the psalmist, the children of men find refuge in the shadow of God's wings; they feast on the abundance of his house, and they drink from the river of God's delights, for with God is the fountain of life (cf. Ps 36: 8–10). "Give me," comments Augustine, "someone who loves, and he will know what I am saying; give me someone who hungers, give me someone who wanders in the wilderness and thirsts and yearns for the source of the eternal home; give me one such man—and he will understand what I am saying. But if I ask someone hard-hearted, he won't understand what I am saying."[15]

No doubt: the triune, loving God strives to win man's heart: God desires the individual person to turn to him and abandon himself to him in a loving way. God conducts himself in relation to man like a spiritual guide who shows him the road to eternal bliss. Outstanding individual destinies and extraordinary lives can only be explained in this way. They powerfully testify to the interest God takes in humankind. And they have the persuasive force of exemplary models and the fascination of the authentic; for God's work of salvation is always original and astonishing.

---

[15] Augustine of Hippo, *Io. eu. tr.* 26 (CChr. SL 36,261).

INDIVIDUAL'S NEED FOR THE CHURCH: ERIK PETERSON

The insights of the Fathers of the Church were based on acute spiritual sensibility and their own experience. They ought not to be dismissed as pious legends, for they are confirmed by the experience of our contemporaries—for example, by a man of the last century, a great theologian with outstanding professional qualities who described the story of his own life and whose path has been more recently clarified for us with new biographical information: Erik Peterson († 1960).[16] His meditations, his spiritual confessions, and episodes from his eventful life, tell us how God himself moved his soul and show that the soul of the individual in its response to God's call cannot be represented by others.

It was the *Deutsche Christliche Studentenvereinigung* (DCSV), the German Union of Christian Students, that "psychologically considered"—as he wrote in his correspondence with A. von Harnack—prepared the way for the young Peterson's conversion. This student association whose culture was inspired by the German tradition of Pietism, saw its goal as leading young men and women to share the experience of "rebirth." Contemporary Christianity seemed atrophied in its social application to the young people of the time. In spite of that, according to the witness of Holy Scripture, God looked to the baptized for an individual and personal conversion to Christ and the missionary transmission of the faith to others.

Erik Peterson recounted the experience of his "rebirth" in a brief autobiographical note. The writer's excitement at this experience can still be felt. At the same time, the very specific contents and circumstances of the event, which heighten its credibility, can be grasped by the reader. Clearly for Peterson the beatific meeting with God was preceded by a long period

---

[16] For an excellent profile of Peterson's life and work see Barbara Nichtweiss, *Erik Peterson. Neue Sicht auf Leben und Werk*. Freiburg, 1992; the page numbers interpolated into the text refer to this biographical account.

of painful interior and exterior turmoil: he speaks of the end of his struggle and conflict. Then—he is quite specific about the time and the place—the beatific experience was granted to him. It sprang not from meditation on Scripture, but more probably from his profound effort to grasp the nature of the Trinity, since we cannot help being struck in his account by the repeated mention of each of the three divine Persons. These Persons "showed" themselves. Their revelation triggered Peterson's conversion, which is described with great self-awareness and emotional force: he speaks of his emotions of joy, happiness, and the "sweet feelings that filled his thoughts."

The event of his conversion gave Peterson a certainty he had long craved, and this too is mentioned repeatedly. In addition, he was filled with praise of God, which continuously urged his lips to speak and his voice to utter it aloud; it strikingly took the form of a kind of glossolalia. At the same time, he could not contain his gratitude—for this experience of conversion, but also for Christ's work of salvation, which he could now appreciate as a fact that personally involved him. He knew, however, that this experience was not yet heaven; he speaks of the prospect of further struggles and the snares of Satan:

> Lord God, my dear, dear Father. From the depths of my heart I thank you for having revealed yourself to me today, through your Holy Spirit and our Lord Jesus Christ, your only begotten Son. How can I thank you, Father, for this goodness of yours! The struggle and conflict are now at an end. You have now become my beloved Father and Jesus my dearest Brother. My Jesus (Lord), remain at my side as my protector, for Satan will often come back to me. Then let us fight side by side against him.
>
> How joyful I am, how happy I am, that I have now been reborn. My new life dates from today, 7 July 1910 (Tuesday).
>
> It was evening. As was my habit, I went for a walk. Once again I was racked with doubts, unable to be wholly certain of God and also of Jesus, though they were still the goal of my

wishes and I had continued to deceive myself into thinking I already possessed them. But then God sent me his Holy Spirit. A sweet feeling of gratitude arose in my mind. God possessed my heart and I had become conscious of Jesus. How great was my joy! The whole way back home on my walk I praised God with my tongue and thanked my beloved Lord Jesus for having accomplished the bitter task of coming into the world and dying for us. I am now conscious of everything the Church teaches and everything that the living members of the Church have felt.

Now that the Spirit of God has been given to me I know why Christ, God and man, died for us, why the Trinity exists and what it is, because now I have experienced it. I am happy. A thousand thanks to you, Lord, Lord, my eternal Father, my Jesus made strong by the Passion, and the Holy Spirit (64 f.).

The student Peterson had this experience under the influence of the DCSV. The writings and life of the Danish philosopher Søren Kierkegaard also had a strong lifelong influence on him. This philosopher is amply represented in his private library, which in part goes back to his student days (69). Looking back on his spiritual development, he identified the great defender of the individual as his "spiritual mentor," whose capacity for reflection had "perhaps preserved him from his worst errors" (99). Kierkegaard's keywords "despair," "passion" and "decision" were for him an important source of inspiration and motivation, especially in the years following the First World War (99–143). Yet Peterson's spiritual quest and thinking increasingly led him beyond the lessons of his mentor.

And it is just this perseverance in his striving for truth that reveals a further element of particular importance for our present reflection. In contrast with the Dane, according to whom the Church could never produce any qualitative improvement in the life of the individual, Peterson, despite all his criticisms of the failings of his Church, never lost sight of the close community that bound together the faithful in the Church. This can be deduced from lines written to an unnamed "friend," presumably written around 1918/19 (123). Peterson refers here to the Letter to the Ephesians, in support of his argument that the truth is not something single, and empirical, limited to a particular object, but is brought into the world, and expressed in real events by manifestation and revelation. "Only thus is it possible to explain the link between the Church and the founder of the faith, [...] for this link is not of a secondary nature, as maintained by Protestantism and liberalism, but lies in the very nature of religious communication (indirect communication: for Christ—since his being is divine—can only speak through the mouthpiece of men, i.e., through the Church) and is founded upon the very nature of truth (truth can only be grasped in existence—i.e., in human experience—and not in logic)" (162).

It would of course be fascinating to enlarge here upon the justification for Peterson's attacks on theological knowledge—a late echo of the DCSV's influence on him. But for our purposes what is of particular interest is the importance that Peterson, even when still a Protestant, gave to the Church: it guarantees to the individual a living bond with Christ. Kierkegaard had felt himself particularly attracted by Luther's *pro me* gospel of salvation and had therefore favored an individualistic perspective, but Peterson never lost his conviction of the individual's need for community and thus proclaimed the need for the Church as source of *communio*. Referring once again to the Letter to the Ephesians, he placed in close proximity to each other "the existence of Jesus Christ and the existence of the (community) of his successors" and explicitly underlined that this link was not "secondary" (162). His conversion to the Catholic Church was finalized on December 23, 1930.

MOTIVATED BY FELLOW-BELIEVERS: CHARLES DE FOUCAULD

Erik Peterson's long and hard-won journey of faith is an important point of reference for those who wish to explore the individual and communal presuppositions for the maturation of faith and the forging of an individual and personal relationship with God. The theologian teaches that the individual needs the Church for the concrete meeting with the truths of the faith—irrespective of the fact that the content of the faith is not something freely available to everyone in the marketplace. God's ineffability—however paradoxical it may seem—is also communicated through the Church.

This interpretation, however, is far from uncontested. Thinkers and theologians of the Protestant tradition do not share it. The German Protestant theologian Ernst Troeltsch, for instance, maintained that communities are superfluous concessions to human needs. There is, he argued, a religious illumination which is the immediate manifestation of the work of the Spirit, whose presence is one and the same in all things and whose reception is always an individual experience. He called the category of Christian existence thus defined "mystical individualism." Yet the system of categories elaborated by Troeltsch remains a mere academic speculation with no persuasive power. The lives of seekers of God, by contrast, provide us with abundant evidence of the individual's need to be linked to a community. This contributes in a decisive way to the existential encounter with God.

Charles de Foucauld († 1916), the French priest, student of Islam, and missionary in the Sahara, testifies to this. A prayer he penned during his spiritual exercises in Nazareth on November 8, 1897 describes how God lovingly reached out to him. It consists of more than 8,000 words written in a single day. They comprise a triumphal hymn to God's compassion and love: God is the savior; giver of all gifts; the real lord of life. The soul of the humble domestic servant in a convent of Poor Clares—which Charles de Foucauld had become in Nazareth—is full of penitence and jubilation; he reviews his own past with gratitude and prayer.[17]

---

[17]The text of the prayer can be found in: Charles de Foucauld, *Immer der letzte Platz.* München, 1975, 101–121. On Charles de Foucauld's life as a humble servant in the convent of the Poor Clares in Nazareth cf. Anne Fremantle, *Desert Calling. The Life of Charles de Foucauld.* London: Hollis & Carter, 1950, 164–175.

The high point of his "profession of faith" was undoubtedly his experience of conversion: for it was then, in the very moment of conversion, that he experienced God's benevolent turning to the tormented and despairing searcher for truth. But Brother Charles also discovered God in the circumstances, the daily realities, both large and small, that led to this decisive turning point of his life, and especially in his relationships with members of his family and with friends and companions. They showed him the way, and so God revealed himself to him and gave a meaning to his life.

He often mentions his childhood in Strasbourg; for it was his mother who had first spoken to him of God. He thinks nostalgically of his visits to church as a boy, the practice of decorating the cross, the private altar at which he had worshipped, the day of his First Communion. The example and the words of his devout grandfather recur to him. After the excesses in the military academy of Saint-Cyr, the cavalry school of Saumur, and (following his resignation as a cavalry officer) his explorations in Morocco, de Foucauld returned to the bosom of his family in Paris in February 1886. That aroused in him new zest for life. "Two angels," his aunt Madame Moitessier and his cousin, Marie de Bondy, brought back to his mind memories of his own childhood (115 f.). The younger, in particular, led him, though more by example than by word, to question his life: since she was a highly intelligent girl, the religion in which she believed so firmly could not be the nonsense it was commonly thought to be.

In October 1886 Charles de Foucauld experienced a hunger for God hitherto unknown to him. He visited churches and prayed to God, dark though God's presence still was to him, to reveal himself. Again and again he prayed: "God, if you exist, make yourself known to me." The content of the faith also aroused his interest. Presently he met the heaven-sent priest (and Marie de Bondy's confessor) Abbé H. Huvelin, who brought God's work to a first conclusion: one morning towards the end of the month Charles entered the church of Saint Augustine (the parish church of which the abbé was rector) and found the priest, whom he was meeting for the first time, in the confessional. He told him he had not come to confess, since he had no faith; he only wanted to get to know the Catholic faith better. The abbé ignored his words; he simply said: "Kneel down and confess." Then he administered Holy Communion to him.

Reception of the sacrament and inner certainty of the presence of God go hand in hand. The meeting with God is prepared and transmitted through the witness and action of members of the Church, whether ordained ministers or not. The community dimension of the work of salvation then comes into its own. That does not weaken the force and momentum of the individually experienced irruption of God into his life. Several years after his conversion, Frère Charles, as he had come to call himself, wrote (August 14, 1901) to a friend, H. de Castries, whose faith was crumbling: "As soon as I believed that there is a God, I grasped that I could do no other than live for Him: my religious vocation came to me at the same time as my faith: God is so great!"

The immediacy of God, who reveals himself to the individual, can undoubtedly become for him like the cry of Archimedes, *eureka* ("I have found it"), a defining moment of God's bursting into his life: in an intimate meeting man is dramatically penetrated by a new certainty of faith and finally discovers the treasure hitherto hidden from him. God may also make use of those who in this way become his tools to give new impetus to communities in the process of being formed or to the Church as a whole.

"VAE SOLI—WOE TO HIM WHO IS ALONE" (ECCLES 4:10)

Paul of Damascus is no doubt the outstanding proof of this truth. His letters and the Acts of the Apostles return again and again to the blinding apparition of Christ that was the defining moment in his life. The two reports of Luke emphasize the exceptional nature of Saul's conversion on the road to Damascus. Although he was surrounded by fellow-Jews, his traveling companions, Christ appears to him alone. According to the first account, "The men who were traveling with him stood speechless, hearing the voice but seeing no one" (Acts 9:7). According to the later version, recounted by Paul himself, "those who were with me saw the light but did not hear the voice of the one who was speaking to me" (22:9). It is precisely the contradictions of these two versions that make clear the evangelist's intention to set apart the receiver of the revelation from his traveling companions: In his encounter with the Risen Lord, Paul is the individual who stands alone, isolated in his individual experience. The revolution of his life, the radical new beginning that the revelation of Christ triggers in him, at first involves him alone. From that time on, time begins to be measured by him in a different way. It changes not only his relationship with God, but also all his previous experience: with the phrase *"apo tou nyn*—from now on" (2 Cor 5:16) he describes the moment in which his knowledge of Christ, his way of thinking and acting, are fundamentally transformed.

Yet the vision of Christ that Paul so clearly had as an individual and that so clearly was directed to him alone, did not occur in a vacuum, to the exclusion of the Christian community. For the Risen Lord, soon after appearing to Saul on the road to Damascus, brought the apostle he had chosen into the company of Ananias, the representative of the young Christian community in Damascus. Told by the Lord in a vision where Paul could be found, Ananias entered the house where he was staying, and prayed over him. Immediately Paul was filled with the Holy Spirit and his sight was restored to him, enabling him to "see" that Christ was the reason for his personal salvation (Acts 9: 10–19). Only then does Paul strive to harmonize his apostolic mission with the Church; it is the Church that first confirms him in his mission and gives him the certainty that he is not "running or had run in vain" (Gal 2:2). That Paul "had received the Gospel and the apostolate through the Revelation of Christ" was evidently not enough to sustain his conviction: he needed the confirmation of the community. "Precisely because this is undeniably the case, the unity of the Gospel and of the apostolic ministry must be corroborated by the relationship between him and the apostles that preceded him."[18]

After the apostle of the Gentiles, it remains for me, lastly, to mention Martin Luther, in order to elucidate one further aspect of man's relationship with God. It is not that the father of the Reformation was necessarily the best interpreter of Pauline theology, but because he dispensed with the tension inherent in the relationship between the individual and the community. In contrast to Paul, Luther lost himself in an extreme individualism that led him to seek God outside the Church.

In Luther's life, too, there was a defining moment that triggered his conversion. It too occurred "on the road" (the road in this case to Erfurt). He experienced it during a violent thunderstorm on July 2, 1505, when a bolt of lightning struck the ground just beside him. Luther directly attributed this traumatic shock to God, but the God who thus burst so violently into his life is not, in this case, the loving and benevolent Father, but a punitive and vengeful God; a God who even demands what man is unable to give him. So Luther was seized with terror. It was terror he felt when, in the darkness, he suddenly saw two demonic eyes staring at him and became conscious that this moment would cost him his life.

This experience further isolated Luther from all his fellow-believers. His sermons in 1522 make this isolation clear: "Each individual must see himself in his own dugout and fight his own fight, and battle against his enemies, the devil and death, alone; for then I shall not be with you, nor you with me."[19] And on another occasion he declared:

> You [the Pope] will not struggle for me, nor will you give answer
> for me when I should die, because I must understand alone how
> to become as certain of the Word of God as you yourself are,
> or perhaps even more certain than you can imagine. Even if all

---

[18] Heinrich Schlier, *Der Brief an die Galater*. Göttingen (11th edition), 1951, 36f.

[19] Martin Luther, *Opera omnia*, Weimar Edition (WA), 10 III, 1ff.

men were to come, and the angels too, to judge—you cannot reach the verdict yourself, you cannot sit in judgment over yourself, so you are lost [...] For when on your deathbed you want to say: The Pope said that, the Councils decided that, the Holy Fathers [...] determined that, then the Devil will soon bore a hole and break in, saying: What if it's all false? Could you not have made a mistake? [20]

For Martin Luther, it was only a logical consequence of the self-isolation into which he had dug himself that, pressed by the Diet of Worms to explain his theses, he could only reply: "For it is difficult, unholy, and dangerous to act against conscience. God help me, Amen!"[21]

Such logic clearly shows that Luther's overestimation of his own person had blinded his judgment. For why then does Luther not ask himself the opposite question: "May not I err if I continue to seek certainty in myself alone?" This attitude conceals far more than simple self-deceit. The implications of his thought are more dramatic, even explosive; since such an extreme form of egocentrism acts as a kind of ecclesiological declaration of war. Protestant scholars of the caliber of Werner Elert have asked themselves whether Luther had perforce to become the destroyer of the Church. In any case, Luther's position marked the extreme limit of the individual in his search for God.

"BURIED WITH CHRIST" AND "RAISED FROM THE DEAD WITH CHRIST"

Our meditation on the believer as an individual, and his relation to the community, first focused on the subtle observations of the Fathers of the Church concerning God's inner guidance of man. Astonishing and dramatic events in the midst of our everyday life—such as what happened to Saint Paul on the road

---

[20] Ibid., 259f.

[21] Cited in Erwin Iserloh, 'Martin Luther und der Ausbruch der Reformation,' in *Hd KIV*, Freiburg, 1967, 3–144, here 80.

to Damascus—could then testify to the fact of God's bursting into human life. Our investigation should therefore arouse new certainty in all pastors that the Almighty is close to the life of each individual person and shows loving interest in each. It should encourage the pastor to direct new attention to God's manifestation in each Christian soul, even if he might have preferred practical rules that he could directly apply to his pastoral and catechetical work.

For many reasons, however, it is not possible to furnish such rules here. Perhaps no such curriculum exists, no such "instructions for use" telling how to experience God. Today, in particular, we must react against such exaggerated expectations. It is precisely because the reigning spirit of our time suggests the feasibility of all our aspirations and desires that the current "production models" for the experience of God are so deceptive.

So I propose to conclude simply by drawing attention to some pointers, a few basic precepts or axioms for learning and teaching the capacity for the "inner hearing" of the voice of truth to which Pope Benedict XVI referred in his homily quoted at the head of this chapter.

I. From a pastoral point of view, the urgent need for a "mystagogy"—an interpretation of the mysterious way God works in the individual soul—cannot be doubted. Anyone who sees no task for the Church in this does not know the soul of the contemporary Christian. "The primary and essential element, which must also characterize the devotion of the future, is the personal and direct relationship with God. [...] The devout Christian of the future will be a 'mystic,' someone who has 'experienced' something, or he will no longer exist at all," wrote Karl Rahner immediately after the Second Vatican Council.[22]

2. In conformity with the reigning anthropocentrism in apostolate and evangelization, the Church's pastoral ministry must

---

[22] Karl Rahner, 'Frömmigkeit früher und heute,' in: *Schriften zur Theologie* VII. Einsiedeln, 1966, 11–31.

not overlook the need for individual pastoral care and for God to be experienced by the individual person. The guidance given by the patristic sources in this sense is theologically reliable and can furnish useful stimuli. The image that occurs to me is that of Michelangelo's Adam in the newly restored frescoes on the ceiling of the Sistine Chapel: his powerfully outstretched finger graphically brings home to us that man cannot live without God.

3. The Christian must be convinced that God has already found him. The Christian bears "God on his back"—not as a possession to be hoarded, but as a gift to be handed on: to share with fellow-Christians what God has already done for him: to reveal to his fellowmen God's love and his Gospel of salvation. In this sense the experience of God means acting hand in hand with God to bring his Gospel to our brothers and sisters—not turning one's back on the world, but going out into the world to spread the Gospel in deed and in word. Pope Benedict XVI's first encyclical *Deus Caritas Est* brilliantly and convincingly highlights this connection of personal faith and charity to man: "the unbreakable bond between love of God and love of neighbor" (no. 16).

4. The happy experiences of our life: in love and friendship, in the satisfactions of our careers, and in the inner renewal bred of the meeting with nature will give us an authentic "taste for God." Yet it is not only the agreeable moments, the moments of pleasure and diversion, that represent an occasion for loving others with God. The cross and the experience of being utterly forsaken are inseparable from God's love in Jesus Christ. They will also lead the person who loves others with God into the darkness and into a world of suffering, so that he may "find God" at the foot of the cross. The three witnesses we mentioned above, Erik Peterson, Charles de Foucauld, and Paul of Tarsus, were led, with "God on their backs" to the experience of God in total self-oblation.

5. The motto of Saint Ignatius of Loyola was: "Find God in all things." In his "Contemplation to Attain Love" (Exercises nos. 230–237) he writes of God's benevolence, "all the great good he had received" from God; it had "stirred him to profound gratitude" and had led him "to ponder with deep affection how much God our Lord has done for me, and how much he has given me of what he possesses" (no. 234). At the same time, Ignatius had before his eyes that this goodness of God himself also comprised "the great suffering and sorrow" of his Son, contemplation of whom fostered "an attitude of sorrow, suffering, and heartbreak" (no. 206).[23] But just this communion with the suffering Christ permits man to participate in his Resurrection: as we were "buried with Christ," so we shall be "raised from the dead" with Christ (cf. Rom 6:4).

---

[23] Ignatius of Loyola, *The Spiritual Exercises and Selected Works*, edited by George E. Ganss, S.J. New York: Paulist Press, 1991, 169–170, 176–177.

INDEX OF NAMES

❧